MACABRE MONTREAL

MACABRE MONTREAL

Ghostly Tales, Ghastly Events, and Gruesome True Stories

Mark Leslie & Shayna Krishnasamy

DUNDURN
TORONTO

Cover image: © Shayna Krishnasamy
Printer: Webcom

Library and Archives Canada Cataloguing in Publication

Leslie, Mark, 1969-, author
    Macabre Montreal : ghostly tales, ghastly events, and gruesome true stories
/ Mark Leslie, Shayna Krishnasamy.

Includes bibliographical references.
Issued in print and electronic formats.
ISBN 978-1-4597-4258-1 (softcover).--ISBN 978-1-4597-4259-8 (PDF).--
ISBN 978-1-4597-4260-4 (EPUB)

    1. Ghosts--Québec (Province)--Montréal. 2. Haunted places--Québec
(Province)--Montréal. I. Krishnasamy, Shayna, author II. Title.

BF1472.C3L473 2018   133.109714'27   C2018-904100-5
                                                     C2018-904101-3

1 2 3 4 5   22   21   20   19   18

We acknowledge the support of the **Canada Council for the Arts**, which last year invested $153 million to bring the arts to Canadians throughout the country, and the **Ontario Arts Council** for our publishing program. We also acknowledge the financial support of the **Government of Ontario**, through the **Ontario Book Publishing Tax Credit** and the **Ontario Media Development Corporation**, and the **Government of Canada**.

Nous remercions le **Conseil des arts du Canada** de son soutien. L'an dernier, le Conseil a investi 153 millions de dollars pour mettre de l'art dans la vie des Canadiennes et des Canadiens de tout le pays.

Care has been taken to trace the ownership of copyright material used in this book. The author and the publisher welcome any information enabling them to rectify any references or credits in subsequent editions.
— *J. Kirk Howard, President*

The publisher is not responsible for websites or their content unless they are owned by the publisher.

Printed and bound in Canada.

VISIT US AT

dundurn.com | @dundurnpress | dundurnpress | dundurnpress

Dundurn
3 Church Street, Suite 500
Toronto, Ontario, Canada
M5E 1M2

For all the ghosts who roam this city, and for those who run from them

Foreword

Montreal, a Haunted Researcher's Paradise

When the sun sets over Montreal, the vibrant city transforms into a dark and shadowy metropolis. As the night cloaks the island, Montreal becomes eerie and ominous. In this macabre urban setting, terrifying tales have long been told. With hundreds of documented ghost stories, Montreal easily lays claim to being the most haunted city in Canada, if not all of North America.

To take advantage of this unique situation, in 2011 I founded Haunted Montreal, a company that researches local ghost sightings, paranormal activities, historic hauntings, unexplained mysteries, and strange legends, and utilizes all this information to conduct ghost walks. With so much material to choose from, Montreal is a haunted researcher's paradise.

Montreal is the perfect city for ghost walks. It is a city of *quartiers*, distinct little neighbourhoods, each with its own unique history and architecture. Incredibly, many *quartiers* have enough ghost stories to create tours. Old Montreal, Griffintown, the old red-light district, Chinatown, Point St. Charles, Centre-Ville, and the Golden Square Mile are all very haunted. Mount Royal also has its ghosts. Many of them originate from the mountain's cemeteries that form the largest intact burial ground in North America. It is a veritable City of the Dead overlooking the City of the Living.

So, Montreal is a wonderful city to explore the mysterious and the macabre. It is also an incredibly beautiful city: its architectural heritage is largely preserved, meaning historic buildings dating all the way back to the 1600s still exist. Walking the streets fills one with wonder — of all kinds.

The city's riveting history reads like a timeline of terror. The island has been inhabited for thousands of years by various Indigenous Peoples. Known in earlier times as *Tiohtià:ke*, the fertile island was a place of trade, diplomacy, and habitation. When the French attempted to colonize the island in 1642 by establishing a settlement called Ville-Marie, the Haudenosaunee Confederacy, a league of five First Nations, was not impressed. A bloody and intense war erupted. The Iroquois War raged on and off for almost sixty years. Captured enemies were forced to endure gruesome forms of torture on both sides of the conflict.

When the British conquered the city in 1760, a whole new type of brutality began, as the Redcoats arrived to impose the power of the British Crown over the French inhabitants. When rebellions broke out in the 1830s, they were crushed under the heels of the British soldiers, who burned down farms in the regions surrounding Montreal, bombarded churches with cannon fire, and hanged patriots at the local prison.

The bodies continued to pile up.

In 1847, tens of thousands of typhus-stricken Irish refugees over-whelmed the city. They had fled Ireland in a bid to escape a devastating famine there. However, conditions aboard the notorious coffin ships were even worse. Deprived of food and water, the poor were crammed into fetid, rat-infested holds where disease ran rampant. Those who survived the trip were confined to camps by the docks, where many of them died.

Not only was there disease and death, political violence was also a problem in nineteenth-century Montreal. Just two years after the Irish influx violent politicians burned down Parliament, causing Montreal to lose its status as the capital.

And the deaths continued.

The Victorian era saw some of the city's most deranged murders, including that of Mary Gallagher, a lowly prostitute who was beheaded by her best friend in Griffintown. During Prohibition in the 1920s Montreal became known as "Sin City" as mobsters took control and began knocking each other off in the red-light district. In the 1960s, deadly terrorist bombs exploded throughout the city, causing local residents to live in fear. Today, things have settled down a bit, but the ghostly traces of the city's unbearably macabre past still remain.

It is the combination of distinct *quartiers*, preserved heritage, and deranged history that makes Montreal the ideal haven for eerie and spine-tingling tales. While most large cities have many books dedicated to their ghost stories, *Macabre Montreal* is a long-overdue first for our metropolis. As a dedicated researcher of Montreal's ghosts and haunted legends, it is my absolute honour to write the foreword to this tome. I hope its stories keep you up at night.

Donovan King
Haunted Montreal

Introduction

I Have Seen Things in the Dark

I have night terrors. About an hour after I fall asleep, I wake up convinced my bedside table is out to get me, or incredibly suspicious of the sweater hanging off the back of my chair. I once thought an exercise bike was trying to kill me and that my bed was full of rats, and that only locking myself in the bathroom would save me. Sometimes I'm able to convince myself it's highly unlikely that hundreds of spiders are marching up and down my bedroom wall, and other times I rise up in my sheets, trembling with fear, sure it's all real. I've woken up with my hand on the bedroom door handle (readying to flee), my entire body drenched in sweat. I've jumped out of bed and run from the room, screaming so loud and long my husband had to slap me awake. I've seen things. Weird things. And they all seemed incredibly real at the time.

It's a strange nightly ritual, one I rarely talk about, because upon waking in the morning the events of the night often seem blurred and far away, dreamlike, unreal. The fact is that when I'm experiencing a night terror I am technically still asleep. I can see the room around me, just through a horror-movie lens. It's like a waking nightmare in which all the everyday things I look at in the daytime come alive at night and try to kill me.

I have also seen people who aren't there.

One time, sleeping over at my then boyfriend's apartment, I looked up and saw a thin wire extending from the window to the top of the bookcase. Then I saw a little man on a little bicycle pedal his way across the room on the tightrope before disappearing. He was pink. Once I saw a hunched old woman staring at me from across the room with hatred in her eyes. She turned out to be a stepladder. On another occasion a demonic face came bulging out at me through a solid wall that I maybe, now that I think about it, shouldn't have painted red.

Each of these experiences is uncanny, a lot like seeing a ghost. I see something, a terrible thing, but once I flick on the light it's gone. I feel a presence in the room with me and have the irresistible urge to run. I panic, without quite knowing why. I stare into the face of someone who shouldn't be there, gritting my teeth, willing them to go.

This isn't real, I tell myself. But I don't quite believe.

I'm not a die-hard believer in ghosts. I've never had an encounter with a spirit. I don't have one of those stories to tell. But I have seen things in the dark. I have known the fear of being in the presence of something inexplicable. And as a result, I've always been attracted to creepy stories, the ones that make the hair on your arms stand on end, the ones where the girl turns around and screams at something only she can see. Because I've been that girl.

I hope you enjoy this series of tales of the ghostly, ghastly, and gruesome from my hometown. I know that Mark and I enjoyed writing them. And most of all, I hope you can put them out of your mind before you go to bed tonight so you can sleep a tranquil, dreamless sleep, uninterrupted by any unwanted visitors. I myself will be going to bed in the suburbs of Montreal with one hand on the light switch, as usual, lying in wait for whatever — or whoever — might come around, ready to scream.

Shayna Krishnasamy

Mary Gallagher and Her Missing Head
Griffintown

It happened in Griffintown.

The area located north of the Lachine Canal, south of Notre-Dame Street, and bordered by the Bonaventure Expressway to the east was once a bustling slum. Now an odd mixture of old industrial buildings and sparkling condos, it once housed a mainly Irish community of families and labourers working for the railways, at the port, and on the construction of the Victoria Bridge. Out of this shanty town comes Montreal's most well-known ghost story: that of a headless ghost named Mary Gallagher, who died in 1879, killed by her own best friend.

Mary Gallagher was a prostitute. Though thirty-eight years old (quite aged for a working girl), she was still quite attractive and didn't have trouble finding clients. According to the Haunted Griffintown ghost walk's account of her story, the events that would lead to Mary Gallagher's demise began rather pleasantly on June 24, 1879. She had gone out with her friend and fellow prostitute, Susan Kennedy, to celebrate Saint-Jean-Baptiste Day, a holiday in Quebec. The town was filled with music and festivities. It was fun; it was also perfect for picking up johns.

Though they were unable to find any male companions at Joe Beef Tavern, they went on to Jacques-Cartier Square and there met a young man named Michael Flanagan. They spent the evening together, flirting and drinking at a local watering hole. Flanagan took a special liking to

Gallagher, and the two decided to leave together. They went to a flophouse, leaving Kennedy on her own and none too happy about being abandoned.

Two days later, in the early hours of June 27, Mary and Michael showed up at Susan Kennedy's house. The two-room house was situated on the second floor of a tenement building at the corner of William and Murray Streets. Kennedy seemed willing to let go of her grudge at the time, for she let the two in, even though it angered her husband (both Susan and Mary were married). Kennedy's husband stormed off.

In his article "How a Dismembered Montreal Sex Worker Became a Sensation, Then a Ghost, and Now a Fading Legend," Patrick Lejtenyi reports that the husband, Jacob Mears, was used to Gallagher dropping by at odd hours, but was furious that she'd brought a man with her this time. Apparently, he hadn't yet come to terms with his wife's profession, or perhaps he just didn't want dirty deeds taking place inside his house. He returned some time later to find all three drinking and his wife alone in a room with Flanagan. Another row ensued, this time due to the drinking, and Mears stormed off again. It's lucky that he did, as he left just in time to miss the murder.

In later testimony, Flanagan and Kennedy did not agree about what happened next. When he was questioned by police, Flanagan remembered finishing a bottle of whisky with the two women, then falling asleep by himself in the front room. When he woke up a few hours later in the middle of the day, he wanted to get a drink with Kennedy but she declined. He got up to leave, and on his way out saw Gallagher asleep in the other room. Everything seemed normal, there was no blood, and in Flanagan's opinion Kennedy seemed a little quiet but calm.

Kennedy's story was very different and often contradicted itself. She claimed she followed Flanagan into the other room, and that the two fell asleep side by side. During her trial she testified that later on that day she heard Gallagher invite another man in for a drink, and also heard them arguing before she fell asleep again. When she woke up hours later, the man was gone and Gallagher was dead. Kennedy said she was horrified when she saw the body and literally fell to the ground, too weak to call for the police. Flanagan, she said, woke up around the same time, saw the body, and ran off, as did her husband when he returned home.

A sketch of the building where Mary Gallagher was murdered, at the corner of William and Murray, 1879.

A different story was reported in the *Montreal Weekly Witness*. According to an article titled "Murdered with an Axe," the policeman who was first on the scene reported the explanation Kennedy gave the day of. When he came in, he said, Kennedy was on the bed pretending to be drunk. She claimed that a man had come into the house early Friday to give her some money. For some reason this angered Gallagher; she and the man quarrelled, and he killed her. The man then washed his hands, told Kennedy not to tell the police, and left. Strangely, Kennedy added that she was glad he'd gotten away, because he was good-looking.

So how exactly did Mary Gallagher die? Whether it was by the hand of one of the three men reported to have been in the house or of her own friend, one thing is for sure: she lost her head in a terribly gruesome way.

The *Weekly Witness* called it "one of the most repulsive murders ever chronicled" and quoted the constable at the scene, an army man, as saying he'd never seen a sight like it. This was the first murder to occur in the city in two years, and the police, it seems, were simply not prepared for this kind of violence. Apparently there was blood everywhere, even on the walls, and for a length of time nobody could find Gallagher's head.

The description of Gallagher's body in the *Weekly Witness* is quite gruesome and detailed. Her headless body, clothed in a thin cotton dress, was lying stomach-down on the floor. One of her hands had been cut off, but this wasn't obvious at first because the arm was caught under the body. There were several jagged cuts at her neck, indicating someone had really been hacking at the head before it came off. The head also had several gashes across the forehead, which the *Weekly Witness* reporter believed might have been the result of the first blow Mary received. Her head and hand were found in a wash basin by the stove.

Susan Kennedy, though clearly a little shaky on the details, never wavered in her claim that she was innocent. Flanagan made the same claim, too.

You might be inclined to feel sorry for Susan Kennedy, who was arrested that very day for the murder of her friend — her profession likely biased the police against her. But before you feel too bad, you might want to know a thing or two about Susan Kennedy. In interviewing her neighbours, the plucky *Weekly Witness* reporter uncovered some interesting tidbits about her. She was known to be a disturber of the peace, and was regarded with terror in the neighbourhood — the reporter never bothered to explain why. She was a drinker and a familiar face to the area's police, who stated that she was difficult to arrest. "Difficult" seems an apt description for this woman — some of her neighbours thought she was insane because when drunk she spoke in a silly manner.

There was also concrete evidence linking Kennedy to Gallagher's death: the day Mary died, a boy, likely the son of the downstairs neighbour, notified a policeman that a woman was dead at 242 William Street. A crowd had already begun to form outside the building when they arrived a good ten hours later — disturbances in Griffintown were hardly their priority. Upon entering the house, the policeman found Kennedy alone with Mary Gallagher's body. She was covered in blood and wearing three dresses, one of which belonged to Gallagher. Kennedy tried to explain this away by saying she'd slipped in the blood as she tried to clean it up. A small axe, normally used to chop firewood, was found inside the apartment, covered in blood and bits of flesh and hair. The police examined the body. They examined Mary's head. They arrested Kennedy and Flanagan on the spot.

At Kennedy's trial for the murder of Mary Gallagher, a number of damning pieces of evidence came to light. Lejtenyi writes that one witness claimed to have heard the two women arguing at about midday. Kennedy had been swearing from her window at people down on the street and when Gallagher tried to pull her away she was heard saying, "If you don't leave me alone I'll split your head open with an axe." Not good. The downstairs neighbour testified that she heard a body falling to the floor, followed by chopping sounds. She claimed to have heard Kennedy say, "I've wanted revenge for a long time, and I finally got it." Really not good.

Not surprisingly, Susan Kennedy was found guilty. Though the jury recommended clemency, the judge was in no mood and sentenced her to hang on December 5 of that year — a shocking decision for the time, when it was generally believed that women were incapable of committing murder. Even more shocking was the sentence, for those very few women who were convicted were almost never sentenced to hang.

In a twist of fate, Kennedy did not actually hang. According to John Marlowe's book *Canadian Mysteries of the Unexplained*, Prime Minister Sir John A. Macdonald commuted her sentence to a prison sentence; she would serve sixteen years in Kingston Penitentiary. Strangely, Michael Flanagan, after being acquitted of the crime of murder, slipped while working on a boat in the Lachine Canal and drowned on December 5, the very day Kennedy was meant to hang.

After her time in prison, Kennedy returned to Griffintown, where she lived out the last eleven years of her life. Marlowe states that she was used as a cautionary tale for little children in the area: *Misbehave and Susan Kennedy will get you!* As a result, children were known to leave penny candy at her door to get on her good side.

Mary Gallagher was buried in a pauper's grave, but if the abundant reports about her are true, she did not find her eternal resting place. It's said every seven years since her death she wanders the streets of Griffintown, always visiting the corner of William and Murray Streets, looking for her lost head. The first sighting was on June 27, 1886, Marlowe writes, when her cloaked, headless, figure was seen haunting the streets. Ever since, June 27 has been known as Mary Gallagher Day in Griffintown.

There have been two dozen sightings of Gallagher over the years, though none since the 1920s. This hasn't stopped believers from flocking to her site of her death every June 27, eager to spot her. In 2005 there were nearly one thousand people looking for the ghost with no head, wearing a red dress with green ribbons and black ankle boots.

The building where Mary Gallagher was murdered is long gone. In fact, the corner is currently nothing but an empty gravel lot full of scattered trash, surrounded by graffitied walls. It seems unlikely that Mary's ghost will be seen there again, despite her fame. Perhaps one day, when all the old buildings of Griffintown are no more and the condos and shiny new coffee shops have completely taken over, the story of the headless ghost of Griffintown will fade away, too.

Until then, see you on June 27 at the corner of William and Murray Streets. Don't forget to bring your axe, just in case.

The Tobogganing Ghost of Simon McTavish

Mount Royal

In the late 1700s, Simon McTavish was the richest man in Montreal. An immigrant of Scottish decent, McTavish prospered as a fur trader, founding the North West Company, which would compete for business with the more well-known Hudson's Bay Company, and eventually merge with it. Like many rich men, McTavish was known to be arrogant. He was also somewhat of a dandy, and according to Donovan King, who conducts ghost tours of Montreal, he would strut around town in the finest garments, wearing elaborate jewellery and whacking anyone who disrespected him with a gold-tipped cane. Though he was in no way a nobleman, he insisted on being called "The Marquis."

Perhaps in an effort to literally look down on the inhabitants of Montreal, McTavish purchased a swath of land on Mount Royal, the highest point in the city, right next to a property owned by James McGill. Soon after, in the early 1800s, he began construction of a grand castle for his family, to be built in the Scottish baronial style. As work on the castle neared completion, McTavish liked to stalk around the construction site, striking anyone working too slowly with his infamous cane.

Then fifty-four years old, McTavish would often make the trek up the mountain from his home in Old Montreal on foot. It was on one of these occasions that he was caught in a rainstorm and developed a cold. Being a stubborn man, he would not listen when his doctor instructed him to

The snowshoeing club: Bad boys of the 1800s.

stay in bed to recover and as a result, his cold developed into pneumonia, then pleurisy, and finally killed him just weeks before the castle was set to be completed.

There was an elaborate funeral. A mausoleum was built to house his body and a tall stone monument was erected in McTavish's honour. But work on his beloved castle, so close to being finished, was abandoned. Over the years the structure began to crumble. In an episode of the podcast *Listen with the Lights On*, King muses about how at one point the disintegrating castle resembled a giant hollow skull from the street below as snow collected in the gaping windows, or "eye sockets."

Twenty years later, in 1821, McGill University opened its doors, the crumbling castle looming over its buildings from Mount Royal. It didn't take long for stories to begin to circulate on campus about McTavish, his tomb, and his ghost. These rumours may have been prompted by the school's rabble-rousing snowshoeing club — apparently the bad boys of the 1800s — who liked to get drunk, strap on their snowshoes, light their torches, and run amuck across the mountain. King likens the sight of these boys and their torches going up the mountain to a fiery snake.

Is that a dead man tobogganing in his coffin?

Apparently, this band of mischievous youths liked to make a pit stop at McTavish's tomb to try and rouse his spirit by yelling and carrying-on. On one particularly passionate occasion they even went so far as to break into the mausoleum and vandalize the place, tipping over the coffin and spilling McTavish's remains across the floor.

Simon McTavish's ghost saw its chance and escaped.

It wasn't long before there were reports of ghost sightings at the castle. McTavish's spirit was seen peeking from the doors and windows of the abandoned structure at night. It was even reported that the apparition could be found dancing on the castle roof on moonlit nights. But in perhaps the most Canadian description of a ghost sighting ever reported, McTavish's ghost was spotted tobogganing down the slopes of Mount Royal in his own coffin.

The residents of Montreal became fearful of the mountain after these sightings, and as the castle was a terrible eyesore it was demolished in 1861. To put an end to the desecration of McTavish's gravesite, the rubble from his castle was used to bury his mausoleum for good. During the demolition a construction worker fell three stories to his death, which some believe was McTavish's last act of revenge against those trying to bury his legacy as well as, quite literally, himself.

On the Haunted Mountain ghost walk, King posits a logical explanation for the tobogganing ghost. Though it may not be widely known it was almost impossible to obtain legal cadavers, or corpses, for dissection in the classroom until the mid-1800s. Professors had to get creative in order to teach their anatomy lessons, and it's said that one such McGill professor, nicknamed "The Resurrectionist," did just that. In the dead of night he would climb up Mount Royal to the Catholic cemetery and dig up a corpse from one of the unmarked paupers' graves, which wouldn't be missed, then strap it onto a toboggan and ride down to the medical building.

So we've either got a grave-robbing and possibly unhinged professor of medicine, or a dead millionaire out for a joy ride down the slopes of the mountainside he once considered his. Personally, we know which story we're sticking with. There's nothing more Canadian than a tobogganing ghost, after all.

Ghosts of the Old Royal Victoria Hospital

Golden Square Mile

Spirits of former patients, the echo of footsteps and voices down deserted corridors, lights flickering on and off all on their own, and nurse call buttons being activated with nobody in the room to press them: these eerie events have all been reported in the Royal Victoria Hospital. Though it moved to a new location in 2015, the original buildings of the "Royal Vic," as it has been affectionately known, have been an iconic city landmark near the bottom of Mount Royal. It has links to doctors such as Lieutenant Colonel John McCrae (author of the beloved Canadian war poem "In Flanders Fields"), and was the site of the first injection of penicillin and the first kidney transplant in the Commonwealth.

The Scottish baronial–style hospital was originally built in 1893. It was lauded as one of the finest and best-equipped hospitals in North America and was intended by its founders "to be for the use of the sick and ailing without distinction of race or creed."

Over the years, the hospital has received worldwide recognition for the multitude of positive work done out of it, but not everyone has been so kind in their descriptions of the original hospital buildings. Indeed, Jolene Haley, an author and writer at the Midnight Society, said that the place offered "a creepy Arkham Asylum vibe." Haley's reference to the fictional psychiatric hospital made popular through the Batman comics

The original buildings of the Royal Victoria Hospital, sitting near the bottom of Mount Royal, are an iconic city landmark.

might, of course, be alluding to the hospital's links to the Allan Memorial Institute and the controversial secret brainwashing experimentation that took place there in the 1950s and early 1960s (see "Unspeakable Torture and Mind Control"). Or, Haley may have been referring to some of the other dark tales associated with the Royal Vic prior to the 2015 relocation of the hospital to the Glen site of the McGill University Health Centre (MUHC).

A few of those tales appear in an October 2013 posting on the MUHC'S website. The first tells the story of a nurse who experienced something eerie in the staff room. During a break on one of her long and tiring overnight shifts, she headed to the staff room to take a quick nap on the couch. At one point during the nap, she opened her eyes to see an odd, white smoky substance floating in the air just a foot or so above her. She rubbed her eyes, not sure what she was looking at, and tried to focus on the hazy vision; that's when she realized the transparent wisps of white were in the shape of a person standing over her.

A chill ran down her spine as she slowly sat up and slid her legs to the floor. "Go away," she said quietly. But the smoky figure remained where it was.

The nurse carefully reached toward the figure, but her hand went right through the smoke. As she moved her hand back and forth, the figure and the foggy wisps in the air began to disperse. She sat there, wondering where the smoky haze could have come from and curious if she was hallucinating due to being overtired. She contemplated lying down for a bit longer and getting some more rest.

That's when the foggy figure rematerialized … except this time it wasn't alone. There were two other similarly sized human shapes formed out of white wispy haze standing with it.

Too frightened to scream, the nurse slowly stood and left the staff room. She never saw any of the three smoky figures, or anything remotely similar, ever again. But she did confirm that no matter how tired she was during a long shift, she was never tempted in the slightest to lie down on that couch again.

Another tale concerns a painting of a beautiful house and sur-rounding landscape that once hung on the wall in the Ross Pavilion. It was well liked, part of the relaxing ambiance of the space. But every once in a while when somebody was looking at the painting, small things about it would change. Sometimes there appeared to be an old woman peering out from one of the home's windows. Other times she came out of the doorway of the house, stood there, looked around, and then went back inside. The old woman appeared enough times that people began to complain, and speculation led to the painting eventu-ally being removed from the wall.

What happened to the painting once it was taken down was never revealed.

A former staff member shared her tale about a patient who passed away in the M5 cardiac ward of the hospital. After declaring the man's time of death, the staff carefully arranged his body, left the room, closed the door behind them, and waited for the man's family. When the family arrived, the staff tried to let them into the room, but they found the door bizarrely locked *from the inside.*

Security was called. After they unlocked the door, they confirmed that there was nobody else in the room other than the recently deceased patient. The staff member who shared the story speculated that perhaps the man who had passed away had not been comfortable with his family seeing him in that condition.

* * *

A woman who identified herself only as DB (who we will call "Debbie") posted her story about the Royal Vic on the Haunted North America website.

In 1996, Debbie was spending the night in hospital after a surgery. She woke up in the middle of the night and was shocked to discover she was lying in a large pool of blood, her pyjamas and the bed sheets completely soaked with it.

Horrified by the sight, and fearful that her stitches had opened in the middle of the night, Debbie rang for the nurse. When the nurse arrived, Debbie was beside herself with fear and anxiety, sickened by the feel and sight of all the blood on her clothing and skin.

"One nurse came, then a second, then a third," Debbie wrote. "They were baffled. My bandage was intact, no blood anywhere on my skin. So they decided to remove my bandage, thinking perhaps there was a leak somewhere around it. Once they removed it everything was fine. I wasn't bleeding from anywhere, it was so very strange. My entire body showed no sign of blood at all, yet my pyjamas and bed was full."

Later, during tests, it was discovered that Debbie was anaemic and needed two pints of blood transfused. Debbie speculated that the appearance of the mysterious blood was an omen about her condition.

A short time later, Debbie became frustrated by her long post-surgery recovery stay, reflecting on her scheduled release date and how far away it was. To alleviate her anxiousness, she took a morning walk down one of the corridors, longing for the end of the lengthy hospital visit that seemed never-ending. As she was reflecting on this, she looked over to her right and noticed another patient that she didn't recognize. The older woman was standing in the doorway of one of the rooms and looking directly at Debbie, her frail hand clutching a tall intravenous pole. Debbie wondered if she was newly admitted.

The old woman smiled at Debbie and said, "You really want to get out of here, don't you?"

Debbie was inexplicably chilled by the woman's presence and found herself unable to utter a single word in response. This stranger appeared to know exactly what Debbie had been thinking.

As she glanced down the hall toward the nurses' station, another odd notion struck Debbie. "A strange feeling went through me, like, I just knew I shouldn't be replying.... I just felt this," Debbie shared. "For some strange reason I knew I shouldn't be talking to her. The nurses' station was close by and it was more like a feeling that the nurses shouldn't see me 'talking' with her."

Much later Debbie realized her real worry had been the idea of the nurses seeing her talking to nothing.

Still not saying anything to the woman in the doorway, Debbie quietly nodded her head in acknowledgement.

"Straighten your back," the old woman said, "and walk as fast as you can to the nurses' station. It's going to hurt, but then you'll be out in no time."

Debbie looked at her, considered the suggestion, and contemplated the dozen or more steps it would take to do exactly what the stranger said. Then she took a deep breath, pulled her back as straight as she was able to manage, and walked as quickly as she could past the nurses' station. Though pain shot through her body with every single step, she managed to complete the task. A few hours later, Debbie's doctor came with the good news that she was healing quickly and would be released from the hospital early.

Debbie never saw the strange old woman again. However, a few months later when she returned to the hospital for a follow-up appointment, the elevator she was on stopped on the floor where she'd encountered the old woman. She hadn't pressed the button for that floor.

The first thing Debbie spotted when the elevator doors opened was the intravenous pole, in the same spot in the doorway where the old woman had been clutching it. Upon seeing it, Debbie shook her head, wondering if there were supernatural forces at play.

Debbie shared her belief that there was some kind of presence in the hospital, appearing in the guises of the old woman and the pool of blood that had coated her, and this presence had constantly been looking out for her.

*　*　*

On April 26, 2015, as part of the Royal Vic's move to its new location, 154 patients were transferred the few kilometres west. It was cited as "the biggest hospital move in Canadian history." The Black Watch Royal Highland Regiment paid tribute to the event in a bagpipe ceremony, as 122 years of operation in the original building came to an end.

The old building itself remains empty, abandoned. And though the McGill Campus Planning and Development webpage mentions an ambitious plan to transform the site into a world-class pavilion dedicated to the study of research of sustainable development and public policy, none of the plans for repurposing the old building have come to fruition. A special report by Salimah Shivji of CBC News indicates that the MUHC is on the hook for 7.5 million dollars of annual costs for heating and maintenance of the vacant buildings. One of the methods used to help offset the costs is to allow film companies to use the buildings for a nineteenth-century hospital setting. The MUHC has accommodated filmmakers by keeping several of the rooms filled with old medical equipment.

The dead buildings have also been the birthplace of other creative works. A *Montreal Gazette* article from November 2017 by Susan Schwartz entitled "Portraits of Montreal's Now-Empty Royal Victoria Hospital" describes an art show called Entr'Acte, which is a nod to the fact that the hospital is "between vocations." One of the portraits, entitled "Diane's Escape," by Marie-Jeanne Musiol, is an image named for someone Musiol accompanied on her journey from this life. Marie said she knew she wanted her image to reflect a personal approach and not something that was strictly architectural. "My work has always been about energy and capture of energy in various places," Musiol said. She found that energy while searching in a tenth-floor room in what was once the breast centre of S Block. She came across an intravenous pole in the basement and taped the tubing to the window in the tenth-floor room. "It is the representation, in a certain way, of life going out of the body.... I see the tubes and the swirls as representing the various convolutions of life and death. And finally, the little tube goes out through the window. And the other window is something of an escape route, giving insight into a dimension beyond."

In the fall of 2017, CBC Radio Canada sent Hugo Lavoie on assignment to explore the Old Royal Victoria Hospital for a French language segment of *Gravel le matin*. The piece he recorded is entitled "Visite du tunnel de la mort de l'ancien hôpital Royal Victoria" ("Visit to the Tunnel of Death at the Old Royal Victoria Hospital"). A February 2018 article entitled "Old Royal Victoria Hospital" on the Haunted Montreal blog describes the program about Lavoie's visit:

> The Tunnel of Death connected the hospital to the autopsy room at the Institute of Pathology via an underground corridor that passes under University Street. Interested in recreating the experience of what happens when a patient dies, Lavoie was taken by Dr. Jonathan Meakins, who oversees heritage of the old building, to the former emergency room, the resuscitation chamber, an old surgery room, and through the infamous corridor to the autopsy room.

"It's a bit disturbing," Lavoie explained.

Another reporter, Alyson Grant, a former *Montreal Gazette* journalist, was inspired by some of the stories about the old hospital to write an absurdist play in honour of the building and its ghosts. Her play, *Progress!*, premiered in the fall of 2015 and features two ghosts who, in the tradition of such classics as *It's a Wonderful Life* and *A Christmas Carol*, persuade a suicidal patient, the hospital's very last patient, that her life is worth living after all.

Grant was thinking about the hospital's closure during the year the play premiered and she found herself wondering what would happen to all of the ghosts in a building like that after it is abandoned.

"The original idea of the ghosts being like caretakers was based on something my sister, who was an ICU nurse at the Children's Hospital here, told me," Grant said in a *Montreal Gazette* article. Grant relayed the story of a teenage boy who lay dying in the hospital and received visits from a mysterious red-haired girl who would speak to and comfort him. Yet, despite all the stories the boy shared about this girl, nobody else in the hospital had ever seen her. It was only after the boy died that one of the staff members remembered a young girl with red hair who'd been a patient in the same ward … and who had died there.

"I couldn't help thinking," Grant said, "what's going to happen to the red-haired girl when this hospital is closed? Where is she going to go? What's going to happen to all those other people who died here?"

In a CBC article, Grant spoke about the play and its celebration of the ghosts from the past. "It's my attempt at paying homage to these buildings and to our sense of what they've been in our lives. Many Montrealers have walked these halls and had profound experiences here, either of healing or giving birth, or of death."

Grant is correct. Hospitals are places of healing, places of birth, places of hope. They are also places of trauma, places of suffering, and places of death. Intense emotions and many of the extremes of the human condition are experienced in hospitals. If it is possible for human spirits to be trapped on our earth by trauma or unfinished business, what better location for that to occur than a hospital?

What better location in Montreal than a castle-like building that has stood for more than 125 years, the site of such highs and lows of human experience, and stands, empty and foreboding, overlooking the city below, echoes of the past behind the now-dark windows?

Sleeping Above a Cemetery:
Ghosts of the Grey Nuns Convent
Concordia University Residence

S tudents in the Grey Nuns co-ed residence at Concordia University who are up all night burning the midnight oil aren't necessarily awake because they're cramming for an exam. They may be sleepless because their dreams are plagued with ghastly images related to the building's tragic past, or perhaps because of an unsettling presence they've felt moving through the hallways with them.

Of course, it could be neither of those things.

It might just be the haunting presence of the three hundred bodies buried in the basement.

There are 276 people buried in a crypt below the building, including 232 bodies of the "grey nuns" who were interred there.

The Grey Nuns is the name most commonly given to the order of Roman Catholic nuns originally founded in 1737 by Saint Marguerite d'Youville. Devoted to helping others, the nuns participate in compassionate service, host charitable events, and support society's most vulnerable through schools, hospitals, and long-term care facilities.

By age thirty, Marie-Marguerite d'Youville had lost her father, her husband of eight years, and four of her six children. Instead of letting circumstances overwhelm her, she turned to religion and dedicated herself to helping others. She began by taking the poor into her small home; but, as the group of women who joined her in her efforts slowly grew, they

It might be the presence of the three hundred bodies buried in the basement crypt of this old convent that is keeping some students up all night.

began to take on other projects, and in 1747 they took over the operation of the General Hospital of Montreal.

The term *grey nuns* was derived from the original mocking nickname given to d'Youville and her sisters. The French term *les grises* has a double meaning: both "the grey women" and "the drunken women," the latter a reference to Marguerite's husband, François d'Youville, a bootlegger who had illegally sold liquor to the local Indigenous population. This term stuck and was maintained as a reminder of the group's humble beginnings, even as they grew and continued their important charitable work.

The first Canadian-born saint, Marguerite d'Youville was beatified in 1959 by Pope John XXIII, who called her the "Mother of Universal Charity." She was later canonized by Pope John Paul II in 1990. That same year, in an October 12 *Montreal Gazette* article, Susan Schwartz reported that a plan had been announced by the federal government of Canada in which $851,000 would be invested into the conservation, protection, and internal renovations of the Grey Nuns' former mother house.

This building, which was built in 1871, served as an orphanage and hospital, and, at one point, housed as many as a thousand Grey Nuns. The top floor was used as a dormitory for the young orphans. During the First World War, the lower part of the building's west wing was occupied by sick and wounded soldiers.

On February 14, 1918, a tragic nighttime blaze on the top storey of the building resulted in the deaths of at least fifty-three children (while fifty-three infant bodies were identified, there was speculation in a 2014 *Concordian* article that some children's bodies may have been entirely cremated in the fire).

The Grey Nuns Convent was a place of healing, but it was also a place of death. There were wounded soldiers who never recovered, the children killed in the fire, and the many nuns, young and old, who passed away in the building that was their home.

* * *

In 2004 Concordia University acquired the building from the nuns, which by then had been declared a historic site, and slowly began the process of converting it into a student residence. The last nun in residence moved out in 2013. The high-vaulted chapel in the building was converted to a stately and serene study hall for up to 240 students, and the nuns' rooms were turned into dorm rooms that currently house about six hundred students.

The remains buried in the building's crypt were supposed to have been transferred to Île St. Bernard in Châteauguay, about twenty minutes south of Montreal, which the Grey Nuns own, but Quebec's health authorities refused to allow the opening and exhumation of the tombs, citing health concerns (some of the sisters buried there had died of infectious diseases).

Chris Mota, a spokeswoman for Concordia University, told CBC in April 2013 that the crypt in the basement would be visible to the public, but only returning nuns would be able to visit it. "For the nuns, this was their life," Mota said. "This was home. This was their family. This was where they worked, where they lived.... There's a real connection here, and they will always be welcomed back."

However, in the years since the dorm was converted into a student residence there have been multiple reports of eerie and strange events there that have nothing to do with typical student partying.

In an article for the *Montreal Gazette* in October 2014, Mark Abley reported that one student claimed she was unable to sleep properly while living in the building, regardless of her usual bedtime rituals. She explained that even sleeping pills were not allowing her to sleep through the night. The student's dreams were plagued with ungodly and ghastly images — every time she attempted to close her eyes to sleep, horrific scenes of tortured children being burned alive would haunt her through yet another sleepless night. The student eventually moved out of the residence, claiming it was the only thing that eventually brought the nightmarish visions to an end.

Other student residents shared similarly eerie experiences in an October 2015 article in the *Concordian*. Those experiences weren't restricted to dreams of the horrible 1918 orphanage fire, but involve glimpses of spectres, those who used to live in the building.

"I'm constantly feeling as though I'm sharing my space with other people," Keeara, a Concordia student, said. "There have been multiple times that I have seen both nuns and children walking around corners and standing in the lifts."

The experiences aren't limited to visions and images, but they all include a sense that others are present.

"I haven't had any experiences," said resident Holly, "but I've definitely felt like I haven't been alone in a room."

Kayla, another resident, told CBC that though she hadn't experienced anything she would describe as paranormal she found the building creepy and that there was something eerie in it. "I feel like it's kind of like a ghost hospital," she said.

In an April 2016 interview with CBC, Donovan King, of Haunted Montreal, said that "students moving into residence are literally sleeping above a cemetery, [which is] literally a few metres below. A lot of students get creeped out by this." He said that students have reported hearing the tramping and crying of children coming from the top floor of the building.

According to some daycare workers at the Grey Nuns' residence, a couple of children in the daycare have encountered and played with the same imaginary friend. The spectral playmate matches the description of one of the orphans who died in the 1918 fire and has been described as wearing a tattered hat and ripped, charred clothes.

* * *

There are other, even more ghastly, stories from the convent's past. Some of these tales first appeared in a sensational book first published in 1836: *The Awful Disclosures of Maria Monk*. In the text, Monk claims that Montreal nuns were forced to have sex with priests who entered the convent through secret tunnels:

> One of my great duties was to obey the priests in all
> things; and this I soon learnt, to my utter astonishment
> and horror, was to live in the practice of criminal inter-
> course with them. I expressed some of the feelings which
> this announcement excited in me, which came upon me

like a flash of lightning; but the only effect was to set her arguing with me, in favour of the crime, representing it as a virtue acceptable to God, and honourable to me.

The priests, she said, were not situated like other men, being forbidden to marry; while they lived secluded, laborious, and self-denying lives for our salvation. They might be considered our saviours, as without their service we could not obtain pardon of sin, and must go to hell. Now it was our solemn duty, on withdrawing from the world, to consecrate our lives to religion, to practice every species of self-denial. We could not be too humble, nor mortify our feelings too far; this was to be done by opposing them and acting contrary to them; and what she proposed was, therefore, pleasing in the sight of God. I now felt how foolish I had been to place myself in the power of such persons as were around me.

The book also claimed that if the sexual activity led to a nun getting pregnant, the baby was baptized and then strangled and buried in a lime pit in the basement.

[The Priest] baptized, and then put oil upon the heads of the infants, as is the custom after baptism. They were then taken, one after another, by one of the old nuns, in the presence of us all. She pressed her hand upon the mouth and nose of the first, so tight that it could not breathe, and in a few minutes, when the hand was removed, it was dead. She then took the other, and treated it in the same way. No sound was heard, and both the children were corpses. The greatest indifference was shown by all present during this operation; for all, as I well knew, were long accustomed to such scenes. The little bodies were then taken into the cellar, thrown into the pit I have mentioned, and covered with a quantity of lime.

The book goes on to explain that nuns who did not co-operate disappeared and were never heard from again. Monk claimed that, after having lived in the convent for seven years, the thought of having a child of hers murdered in such a fashion led her to flee, escaping that life.

Some stories about hauntings in the Grey Nun dorm make reference to the disturbing and horrific treatment of the nuns and infants. However, further investigation has revealed that those particular stories might just be fiction.

Maria Monk's sensational book, which is reported to have sold more than three hundred thousand copies by 1860, was later determined to be what today might be called fake news. A March 2017 *Slate* article described the book as a largely successful and "garish package of lies presented to the public as truth for the purpose of swaying political views."

A Protestant newspaper editor from New York, Colonel William Fleet Stone, investigated Monk's claims. He determined after a visit, thorough investigation, and an interview with Monk that there was no evidence to support that she had ever been a resident of the convent.

Regardless of the debunking of Maria Monk's claims, there is no disputing the horrific fire that claimed the lives of more than fifty children, the eerie crypt in the basement, and the ongoing string of stories from students and visitors about unexplained phenomenon.

The real question, posed to you, is this: Given the stories of the building's past and the contents of the building's basement, would *you* be comfortable sleeping — and dreaming — in this dorm?

The Murderer's Cross
Concordia University Residence/The Grey Nuns Convent

Have you seen the large wooden cross on the corner of Guy and René-Lévesque, on the grounds of the former Grey Nuns Convent? At first glance, it seems to be your average Catholic display, with Christ on the cross and religious statues below, surrounded by trees and a garden for quiet worship. The average passerby would hardly give it a second glance. Little do they know that the cross was erected to mark the grave of a murderer buried over 250 years ago.

The Grey Nuns' former mother house is currently being used as a residence for Concordia University students and has its own haunted history (as described in "Sleeping Above a Cemetery"). But in 1752, the land on which it sits was all farmland and a house sat on the spot where the gates to the mother house are now. The farmer was a man named Jean Baptiste Goyer.

According to the story told by Donovan King, Goyer was a lazy farmer who liked drinking at the tavern better than tending to his crops and as a result, his farm was rundown and he never made very much money. In contrast, his neighbours, the Favres, were good, hard-working farmers who did quite well for themselves.

In May of 1752 Goyer decided to take a trip to Quebec City, a voyage that would take a week's time. He told a number of people where he was going before locking up his farm and setting off. Upon his return, Goyer

The cross that marks the spot where Jean Baptiste Goyer is buried.

was horrified to learn that his neighbours, the Favres, had been brutally murdered in their home, their bodies hacked apart. It was apparently a robbery, as all their money had been taken.

Torn up by the deaths of his closest neighbours, Goyer began to spend more and more time at the tavern. He would talk to anyone who would listen about the "unsolvable" murders, and continually suggested that illegal fur traders were the culprits. Goyer believed that they must have crept in from the woods, murdered the unfortunate family, taken their money, and fled back into the forest, never to be seen again. When he ran out of avid listeners, Goyer would start buying rounds of drinks to keep his captive audience. His money never ran out, and the murders were all he would talk about.

His loose lips and spending habits ended up being his downfall. It wasn't long before he became the prime suspect in the case, despite his insistence that he'd been out of town at the time. Soon enough he was arrested.

At the time, torture was freely used to obtain confessions from suspects, and a man nicknamed "The Torturer" — Le Bourreau — was brought in to attend to Goyer. Tying Goyer's hands behind his back, Le Bourreau applied a device called the Spanish boot to the suspect. This instrument consisted of two curved wooden boards, which were tied around the calf in such a way as to resemble a boot. The fit was very snug. Iron spikes or wooden wedges were then hammered between the leg and the boards until the bones of the leg were crushed.

"Did you murder the Favres?" Le Bourreau demanded of Goyer.

"No, I am innocent!" Goyer protested.

But Le Bourreau didn't believe him. In went the first iron spike.

By the time the third spike was hammered in, Goyer was more than willing to make a full confession through tears of pain: He had not gone to Quebec City as he'd claimed. Instead, he'd hidden inside his house until dark. Then he'd stolen across the fields to his neighbour's home with his dagger and pistol. He hadn't meant to murder them, he insisted, only to rob them. But he hadn't moved quietly enough through the house and Jean Favre had emerged from his bedroom to investigate. Upon spotting Favre, Goyer fired on him with his pistol, a non-lethal shot, and Favre and he began to fight. Grabbing his dagger, Goyer stabbed Favre multiple times until Favre's body went completely limp. Of course, the noise of such a battle brought Madame Favre out of the bedroom as well, and so Goyer stabbed her, too, and then grabbed a spade and crushed her skull with it for good measure.

There was no question about it — he was sentenced to death. This time the torture wheel was brought out for the purpose. Goyer was tied to the horizontal wheel and as it turned Le Bourreau smashed at his body with a hammer until he was dead. Goyer's body was tied to a horse-drawn carriage, which dragged him through the streets for a few hours until they arrived at what is now the corner of Guy and René-Lévesque. There they buried him, planting a blood-red cross over his grave. This murderer's cross was erected at a crossroads, as was the custom, to warn others never to commit the same heinous crime.

Years later, when the roads were widened, the cross was moved to its current location. The spot of Jean Baptiste Goyer's actual resting place, then, is likely somewhere under René-Lévesque Boulevard, being run over by cars and trucks for all eternity.

Arthur Ellis and an Accidental Beheading: Canada's Most Famous Hangman

Bordeaux Prison, Ahuntsic-Cartierville

Until 1868 executions in Canada were a public affair, held in a common public area, and attracted huge crowds of spectators. After that, executions were moved inside prison walls, mostly cut off from public viewing (historic reports do, however, reference citizens attempting to watch the ghastly events from the roofs of nearby buildings). Although the executions became a little less out in the open, certain members of the public were still invited in to view the events. That was, at least, until after a horrific 1935 beheading in front of plenty of public witnesses due to a grave miscalculation by Arthur Ellis.

This macabre event not only changed execution protocol, but it also led to the tragic downfall of Canada's most famous hangman, a man who called Montreal home and whose body still rests there.

If you venture to Section N of the Mount Royal Cemetery, you'll find the final resting place of Alexander Armstrong English, known more prominently as Arthur Ellis. English, an ex-army officer, moved to Montreal in 1910 and adopted his working name in a nod to the famous English hangman, John Ellis, after he was recommended to Prime Minster Wilfrid Laurier by British officials. His career was a storied one, however. In an insightful chapter in her book *Drop Dead: A Horrible History of Hanging in Canada*, Lorna Poplak writes that while it is virtually impossible to verify his claims (since record-keeping in the first couple of decades of the twentieth century was not reliable and other Canadian hangmen might have used the same pseudonym), the man claimed to have performed more than six hundred hangings not only in Canada, but also in England and the Middle East.

Regardless of this claim, there is no disputing the fact that the man was kept busy with his macabre role. A *Milwaukee Sentinel* article from 1926 outlines the seven-stop tour between Vancouver and Halifax that Ellis was in the middle of, almost as if he were a musician travelling to awaiting crowds in the various cities.

Ellis took great pride not only in his role, but in the skill that he claimed to possess, such as his ability to quickly assess the weight of the condemned after a quick glance at them. The person's weight was an important factor in a hanging, because it dictated the length of the drop. It's not commonly known that hangings are not intended to cause death by strangulation, which is slow and agonizing. Rather, they are designed to result in the breaking of the convict's neck. The quick drop and sudden snapping action separate the vertebrae, which results in almost instant death. The proper length of rope is integral to achieve this effect. This length is based upon a series of tables that originated in Britain and that hangmen in both England and the Commonwealth relied on. If the length of the rope was too short, the condemned might be strangled to death. If the rope was too long, the condemned might be accidentally beheaded.

This latter result is what happened at Montreal's Bordeaux gallows on March 29, 1935, at the hanging of condemned Montrealer Tommasina Teolis.

Teolis had been found guilty of hiring a hitman to kill her husband, Nicholas Sarao, for a promised five thousand dollars from the man's life insurance policy. The hitman, Leone Gagliardi, and an accomplice named Angelo Donafrio beat Sarao to death. When they were later caught, Gagliardi confessed and all three were convicted and sentenced to death.

But something went wrong with all three hangings.

Ellis first performed the double hanging (not an uncommon thing for him to do) of Donafrio and Gagliardi. Sadly, the length of the rope for both men was too short and neither of them was killed from the drop; instead, they both died slowly and painfully by strangulation.

THE MEASURED DROP OF HANGING

The accidental dismemberment of Tommasina Teolis involved a miscalculation of her body weight. Ellis and other hangmen used a mathematical formula to calculate precise measurements for the lengths of rope used in hangings, which were derived from a series of tables originating in Britain.

After a number of unfortunate hanging incidents in England, Lord Aberdare and the Aberdare Committee created a standardized table of measured drops, or "long drop," which would produce what was called a "striking force" of approximately 1,260 pounds of force, which, combined with the correct positioning of the noose, would result in fracture and dislocation of the neck.

The formula was: 1,260 lbs ÷ [prisoner's weight] lbs = drop (in feet)

The initial table was revised in 1892 to a force of 840 lbs, to reduce the incidents of accidental decapitations, and was again revised in 1913.

ABERDARE COMMITTEE TABLE			1892 TABLE			1913 TABLE		
Weight of prisoner (lbs)	Drop in feet & inches	Ft. lbs. energy developed	Weight of prisoner (lbs)	Drop in feet & inches	Ft. lbs. energy developed	Weight of prisoner (lbs)	Drop in feet & inches	Ft. lbs. energy developed
98	11′5″	1,119	105 & under	8′0″	840	-	-	
112	10′0″	1,120	110	7′10″	862	-	-	
126	9′6″	1,197	115	7′3″	834	118 & under	8′6″	1,003
140	9′0″	1,260	120	7′0″	840	120	8′4″	1,000
154	8′2″	1,258	125	6′9″	844	125	8′0″	1,000
168	7′6″	1,260	130	6′5″	834	130	7′8″	996
182	6′11″	1,259	135	6′2″	833	135	7′5″	1,001
196	6′5″	1,258	140	6′0″	840	140	7′2″	1,003
210	6′0″	1,260	145	5′9″	834	145	6′11″	1,003
224	5′7″	1,251	150	5′7″	838	150	6′8″	999
238	5′3″	1,250	155	5′5″	840	155	6′5″	995

252	5'0"	1,260	160	5'3"	853	160	6'3"	1,000
266	4'8"	1,241	165	5'1"	839	165	6'1"	1,004
280	4'6"	1,260	170	4'11"	836	170	5'10"	992
			175	4'9"	831	175	5'8"	991
			180	4'8"	839	180	5'7"	1,005
			185	4'7"	848	185	5'5"	1,002
			190	4'5"	839	190	5'3"	998
			195	4'4"	844	195	5'2"	1,008
			200 & over	4'2"	833	200 & over	5'0"	1,000

Then, in a example of all the things that could go wrong in a hanging, quite the opposite happened when it was Teolis's turn at the noose.

Her rope's length was too long.

Ellis claimed that the day before the execution, when he went to the prison to see the woman (having claimed all he needed to do was look at someone to quickly determine their weight), the authorities refused to let him visit her, and instead offered him a piece of paper with her weight written on it.

The weight given to Ellis had been the weight she had been when she first arrived at the prison. But she had gained as much as forty pounds while incarcerated, which threw Ellis's rope-length calculation off.

The result was horrific. It gained international notoriety. Newspapers all over North America wrote about that fateful day — when instead of her neck breaking, Teolis's head was torn from her body.

Not only did this gruesome incident result in the ending of public executions in Canada, it also led to the end of Arthur Ellis's career as a hangman.

In a tone befitting a modern tabloid, a *San Antonio Light* article titled "Strange Double Life of Mr. Ellis, Hangman" makes some interesting, if not macabre, claims. The article, with the exceedingly long header of "Respected Canadian Political Figure to His Friends, But Executioner

to the State Until His Wife Discovered His Jekyll-Hyde Life and Left Him
— Then He Bungled His Work, Lost His Job and Has Just Died in Want,"
creates a decidedly dramatic portrayal of Ellis's life that doesn't appear in
many historical accounts.

The article alleges, among other things, that Ellis led a double life,
that even his wife was unaware of his actual job, and that he told her he
was on some sort of "political mission" when he was travelling across
Canada to perform executions. The article states that she left Ellis shortly
after finding out about the secret life he was living.

It goes on to state that, prior to moving to Canada to take up the role
of hangman, Ellis was morbidly interested in prisons and executions;
it was his witnessing of the execution of Mrs. Edith Jessie-Thompson
that inspired him. Thompson was sentenced to her death for the murder
of her husband and had fainted as she was being led from her cell. She
needed to be carried to the gallows in a chair, and was hanged while only
partially conscious. After witnessing that disturbing scene in the yard
at Halloway Jail, Ellis (or Captain English, as he was known at the time)
was impressed by the manner with which John Ellis, England's official
executioner, handled himself and the situation.

The Canadian Ellis did not always handle himself well, however. In
fact, he apparently indulged in excessive drinking — a detail mentioned
in this article as well as several documents about the man's life. The article goes on to state that although Ellis rarely appeared in public and
particularly avoided mixing with people when he was drinking, he did
on occasion venture out — and it was on one such occasion that he was
involved in an incident of public violence. According to the article, Ellis
had been attending a Montreal theatrical performance, sitting "straight as
a ram-rod, a pale, gaunt symbol of death, who must have given an uneasy
feeling to both the audience and the actors. Then, without warning, he
leaped up, whipped out a revolver and started shooting out the footlights."
The article states that it took half a dozen men to subdue him that evening.

It may be that much of this article is speculation, typical of early
1900s tabloid-style journalism, but the picture painted of Ellis could also
be true. In any case, the article certainly shines a dark light on an already
dark element of Montreal's history.

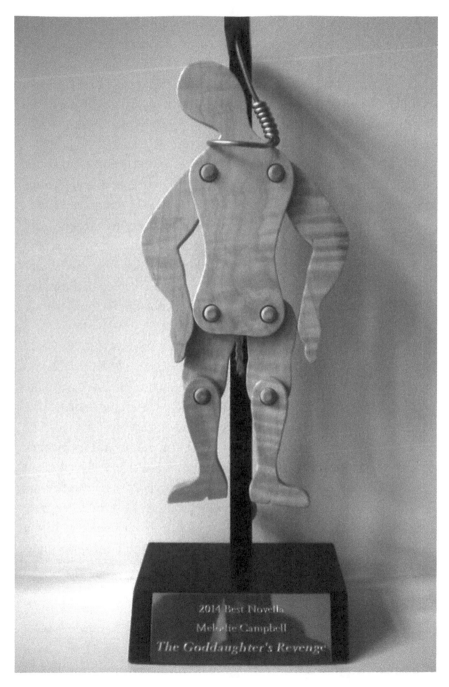

The hanged-man design of the Arthur Ellis Award, named after the famous Montreal hangman.

If he sometimes acted badly in his private life, Ellis was well-mannered in his professional one. His decorum was more than a little disconcerting; in fact, was downright chilling. Ellis, in an interview, claimed that he always smiled at a hanging. Creepy, no? But it's not as macabre as you might think. "Do you realize that my face is the last living thing the murderer sees before he dies," Ellis is quoted as saying. "I try to make his last moments as pleasant as possible."

"Canada's Leading Hangman Proud of His Skill; Has No Distaste for Grim Job" is the headline of a lengthy July 1935 article in the *Evening Democrat*, a newspaper out of Fort Madison, Iowa. In that piece, Ellis is described as a "wizened little man," with keen eyes peering through neat, plain gold glasses, talking cheerfully about the weather in the morning before performing grim executions later that same day. This piece, published shortly after the fateful events in March 1935 that led to the end of Ellis's career serves a kind of epitaph. It appeared before the final chapter of his life, one of decay and downfall.

Sadly, Ellis died alone, miserable, and without a penny to his name. In *Drop Dead*, Lorna Poplak describes how in July 1938, a *Montreal Gazette* article claimed that he had been found in the Ste. Jeanne d'Arc Hospital, emaciated from lack of nutrition and near death. He died shortly after from what was described as an alcohol-related disease.

Less than twenty people attended Ellis's funeral. Even though they had been separated for half a dozen years, Ellis's estranged wife attended and was quoted as describing him as a good man. More than twenty years later, when she too passed on, she requested that she be buried alongside her husband. The two are interred in the Mount Royal Cemetery with a simple headstone that states: "Alexander A. English and Edith Grimsdale. AT REST."

Despite Arthur Ellis's downfall and miserable last days, he lends his name to an annual gala and awards night hosted by the Crime Writers of Canada. The group honours the absolute best of our country's mystery and crime writing during the Arthur Ellis Awards. The trophy, nicknamed "Arthur," comes in the guise of a wooden figure attached to a vertical pole with a noose. Arthur dances and flails when you pull on a string at the back.

Mark Twain's Montreal Telegraphy
The Windsor Hotel

S amuel Langhorne Clemens, better known by his pen name, Mark Twain, was an American writer, humourist, and lecturer. He is often called the father of American literature. Garrulous in person and a prolific writer, Twain could also be private about his feelings and interests. One aspect of his life that he long kept private was his interest in the paranormal.

Like many of his contemporaries, Twain was intrigued and interested in psychic phenomena. However, though he was a member of the English Society for Psychical Research from 1884 to 1902, he was hesitant to broadcast his beliefs in public. Eventually, though, Twain decided to share his thoughts on the subject. In his essay "Mental Telegraphy" he writes in great detail about his belief in the ability for one human mind to communicate with another over great distances. (It is interesting to note that this article was not published until 1891 in *Harper's Magazine* — almost a dozen years after it was written.)

In 1895 Twain published the following article, entitled "Mental Telegraphy Again," in which he writes about an experience he had while visiting the Windsor Hotel in Montreal.

> Several years ago I made a campaign on the platform with Mr. George W. Cable. In Montreal we were honored

with a reception. It began at two in the afternoon in a long drawing-room in the Windsor Hotel. Mr. Cable and I stood at one end of this room, and the ladies and gentlemen entered it at the other end, crossed it at that end, then came up the long left-hand side, shook hands with us, said a word or two, and passed on, in the usual way. My sight is of the telescopic sort, and I presently recognized a familiar face among the throng of strangers drifting in at the distant door, and I said to myself, with surprise and high gratification, "That is Mrs. R.; I had forgotten that she was a Canadian." She had been a great friend of mine in Carson City, Nevada, in the early days. I had not seen her or heard of her for twenty years; I had not been thinking about her; there was nothing to suggest her to me, nothing to bring her to my mind; in fact, to me she had long ago ceased to exist, and had disappeared from my consciousness. But I knew her instantly; and I saw her so clearly that I was able to note some of the particulars of her dress, and did note them, and they remained in my mind. I was impatient for her to come. In the midst of the handshakings I snatched glimpses of her and noted her progress with the slow-moving file across the end of the room; then I saw her start up the side, and this gave me a full front view of her face. I saw her last when she was within twenty-five feet of me. For an hour I kept thinking she must still be in the room somewhere and would come at last, but I was disappointed.

When I arrived in the lecture-hall that evening someone said: "Come into the waiting-room; there's a friend of yours there who wants to see you. You'll not be introduced — you are to do the recognizing without help if you can."

I said to myself: "It is Mrs. R.; I shan't have any trouble."

There were perhaps ten ladies present, all seated. In the midst of them was Mrs. R., as I had expected. She was dressed exactly as she was when I had seen her in the afternoon. I went forward and shook hands with her and called her by name, and said: "I knew you the moment you appeared at the reception this afternoon."

She looked surprised, and said: "But I was not at the reception. I have just arrived from Quebec, and have not been in town an hour."

It was my turn to be surprised now. I said: "I can't help it. I give you my word of honor that it is as I say. I saw you at the reception, and you were dressed precisely as you are now. When they told me a moment ago that I should find a friend in this room, your image rose before me, dress and all, just as I had seen you at the reception."

Those are the facts. She was not at the reception at all, or anywhere near it; but I saw her there nevertheless, and most clearly and unmistakably. To that I could make oath. How is one to explain this? I was not thinking of her at the time; had not thought of her for years. But she had been thinking of me, no doubt; did her thoughts flit through leagues of air to me, and bring with it that clear and pleasant vision of herself? I think so. That was and remains my sole experience in the matter of apparitions — I mean apparitions that come when one is (ostensibly) awake. I could have been asleep for a moment; the apparition could have been the creature of a dream. Still, that is nothing to the point; the feature of interest is the happening of the thing just at that time, instead of at an earlier or later time, which is argument that its origin lay in thought-transference.

It is fascinating to consider Twain's writing about his paranormal experience. The beloved writer and humorist is best known for the riverboat adventures of characters like Huck Finn and Tom Sawyer, but, looking at some of his other works, there is a darker element running through his writing. It's clear that he was fascinated with death, the dead, and even zombies.

Twain's most famous reference to death is his oft-quoted retort to an inquiry about his demise: "The reports of my death have been greatly exaggerated." This is, in fact, a misquote. What Twain actually wrote in response to the 1897 *New York Journal* claim was, "I can understand perfectly how the report of my illness got about, I have even heard on good authority that I was dead. [A cousin] was ill in London two or three weeks ago, but is well now. The report of my illness grew out of his illness. The report of my death was an exaggeration."

Twain also wrote about death and the dead on multiple occasions. His darkly comic play *Is He Dead?* involves an artist whose friends fake his death in order to raise the price of his paintings. The story "A Curious Dream" involves a man witnessing skeletons dragging their coffins down the street, protesting the deplorable condition that the living have let their local graveyard home fall into.

The subject of death is also found in Twain's two most famous works. Tom Sawyer fantasizes about dying and fakes a death by drowning in *The Adventures of Tom Sawyer*. *The Adventures of Huckleberry Finn* includes ghost stories about medical cadavers and a nightmare Pap Finn has about the walking dead.

Clearly Twain was no stranger to writing about the fictional macabre, but it's interesting that it was an experience in Montreal that inspired a real-life brush with the supernatural.

Ghost in the Flames
Auberge Saint-Gabriel, Old Montreal

I t might not surprise you to learn that the oldest inn in North America is haunted. Built in 1688, Auberge Saint-Gabriel has stood for more than three hundred years, during which time a spiteful ghost has taken up residence. Also known for being the first establishment on the continent to get a liquor license, the *auberge* is located in the Old Port, a historic area of Montreal, full of narrow cobbled streets, gas lighting, and old stone buildings that are full of whispers of the past. Come along with me on a trip into Montreal's past to meet Joseph Frobisher, a nineteenth-century fur trader who is a little down on his luck.

In 1809 Mr. Frobisher lives in the building on Saint-Gabriel Street that will one day become Auberge Saint-Gabriel, and he's in need of money. He's made some risky investments, and the bank is knocking on his door looking for payment on his loans. What Mr. Frobisher needs is to make a lot of money, and fast. Lucky for him, when spring arrives and the St. Lawrence thaws, there will be plenty of European buyers looking for furs. The problem is that Mr. Frobisher will be just one seller among many. What he needs is some good luck, or, if luck isn't being handed out, he needs to make some of his own. So plucky Mr. Frobisher does what anyone else would do: he hires the friendly neighbourhood arsonist to help him out.

"Go to the storehouse of my main rival in the fur trade and burn it down," says Mr. Frobisher.

"I'm on it," says the friendly arsonist.

"But make sure nobody is in the building!" Mr. Frobisher adds, hoping the arsonist hears him.

He gets no reply.

The friendly neighbourhood arsonist does as he's told. The building burns and all the furs burn along with it. Though the arsonist burns down the building at night, there are twelve workers in the building at the time and they burn, too.

"What have you done?" Mr. Frobisher cries upon hearing the news. "I told you to make sure no one was harmed! I won't pay you for murder."

The arsonist, still covered in soot from his efforts, is not amused. "You'll pay me and then some," he warns. "A burned building is one thing, I might go to jail. But the murder of twelve people is quite another thing. They'll execute me if I'm caught. I need money to leave town. And I mean right now!"

Seeing he means business, Mr. Frobisher agrees. Rushing over to his desk, he opens the top drawer to take out his money box but instead pulls out a knife. The two men engage in a violent struggle, but in the end Mr. Frobisher manages to stab the arsonist and get away. His escape comes

Auberge Saint-Gabriel, present day. Take note of the infamous window on the right.

not a moment too soon. While neither man was looking, the arsonist's satchel, which holds explosives, falls a little too close to the fire, and moments after his own death the whole building is up in flames.

The explosion rocks the neighbourhood, and everyone comes running. Mr. Frobisher watches in horror as his house is engulfed in flames, not the least because his six-year-old daughter is on the top floor getting a piano lesson from her grandfather. Unable to help them, Mr. Frobisher watches through the windows as his father runs toward the stairs with the girl, but they are already in flames. Desperate to save the child, the old man comes at last to the right-hand window. He opens it and lifts the child up, but the sudden introduction of oxygen into the space creates an instant backdraft. Down on the street, Mr. Frobisher watches as the flames engulf them both.

* * *

Fast-forward 180 years to the late 1980s. The old building on Saint-Gabriel Street has been a private home, a storage unit, a general store, an inn, and now a restaurant and bar. But all is not at peace in this historic building. There's a small storage room in the basement that routinely finds itself on fire. These mysterious fires occur once or twice a month, when nobody is downstairs. When questioned about these fires, a waiter claims that they are somehow starting by themselves. Is this the arsonist, forever trapped in fires he can't escape?

A decade later, more odd happenings. A man is hired to fix the chimney and work on the roof. It's important to note that this man suffers from obsessive-compulsive disorder. He always does his work in the same manner and uses his equipment in the same order. On his first day of work, the man puts down his toolbox and sets up his ladder to the left of it. When he comes back down from the roof, he finds that his toolbox is sitting in a different place, with the ladder to the right of it. He finds this very strange because he *always* puts his toolbox in the same place while working. Puzzled, he brushes off the strange occurrence, moves the toolbox back to its original spot, and continues with his work. Throughout the day, whenever he comes down his ladder, he finds the toolbox has been moved. Suspecting that he's being pranked, the man goes inside and asks the bartender if someone is playing tricks on him. The bartender doesn't know what he's talking about, but he does mention that the building is said to be haunted. Entirely spooked, the worker never comes back and doesn't ask to be paid.

If you're thinking all this paranormal activity is well in the past, think again. In 2008 a local ghost-tracking group reported a piano on the second floor in the *auberge* playing by itself. Photos have been taken of floating orbs on the stairs. The ghost of a gentleman in nineteenth-century clothing has been spotted in one of the dining rooms. And then there is the painting in the dining room, which from time to time is known to display the image of a little girl ... where there shouldn't be one.

* * *

As for Mr. Joseph Frobisher, he doesn't seem to have suffered too terribly from the loss of his daughter. In addition to becoming a successful fur baron, he was elected to Parliament, served in the militia, was a seigneur with 57,000 acres of estates, was a founding member of the North West Company, and also founded the Beaver Club. He died in 1810 at his country home of Beaver Hall, a long way away from Saint-Gabriel Street and the ghosts he left behind.

Books, Blood, and a Ghostly Prankster: The Ghost of McLennan Library

McGill University

O ne would expect to find rare books among the special collections at the McLennan Library at McGill University. But you might be surprised to learn that the collection also houses artifacts of a more macabre nature, such as a bloody cloth ... and at least one spectre sneaking around the stacks.

The fourth floor of the McLennan Library houses the Rare Books Collection as well as Lincoln North, the Joseph N. Nathanson collection of Lincolniana. This collection of more than four thousand items relating to Abraham Lincoln is the largest in the world outside of the United States. Dr. Joseph Nathanson (1895–1989), an alumnus of McGill, amassed items for almost fifty years and donated his unique collection to the university in 1986.

Among the many fascinating items that brilliantly document the life and times of the sixteenth president of the United States, two stand out for their spookiness.

The first is surgeon Charles Sabin Taft's diary. Though this special collection contains thousands of documents, prints, medals, sculptures, and other Lincoln memorabilia that might be found elsewhere, its prized possession is the surgeon's original diary. Taft recorded, in this small notebook, his personal account of the assassination of Lincoln by John Wilkes Booth at the Ford Theatre on April 14, 1865. It recounts the events

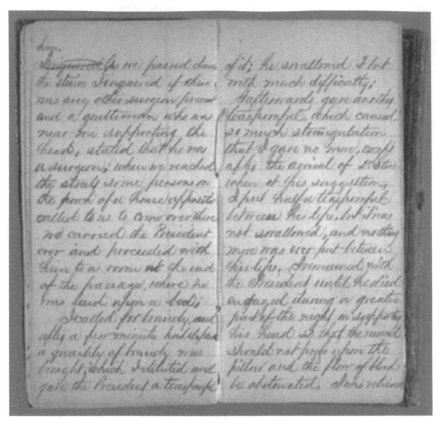

Taft recorded, in this small notebook, his personal account of Lincoln's mortal gunshot wound from John Wilkes Booth at the Ford Theatre.

in the theatre and the efforts, stretching into the wee hours of the next day, of medical staff as they tried to save Lincoln. Finally, it describes the sad moment when President Lincoln succumbed to his injuries.

Taft, who was twenty-three at the time, was the surgeon in charge of the Signal Corps Camp of Instruction at Red Hill in Washington's Georgetown neighbourhood. Though Taft's recollections have been published in many different places and on multiple occurrences, this diary seems to be the only version of Taft's unabridged notes concerning that fateful night and morning.

The fascinating eyewitness account of the shooting and its aftermath appears in a book titled *Abraham Lincoln's Last Hour; From the*

Note-Book of Charles Sabin Taft, M.D. An Army Surgeon Present at the Assassination, Death, and Autopsy, published in 1934 and limited to forty copies. Below is an excerpt.

All went on pleasantly until half-past ten o'clock, when, during the second scene of the third act, the sharp report of a pistol rang through the house. The report seemed to proceed from behind the scenes on the right of the stage, and behind the President's box. While it startled every one in the audience, it was evidently accepted by all as an introductory effect preceding some new situation in the play, several of which had been introduced in the earlier part of the performance. A moment afterward a hatless and white-faced man leaped from the front of the President's box down, twelve feet, to the stage. As he jumped, one of the spurs of his riding-boots caught in the folds of the flag draped over the front, and caused him to fall partly on his hands and knees as he struck the stage. Springing quickly to his feet with the suppleness of an athlete, he faced the audience for a moment as he brandished in his right hand a long knife, and shouted, "Sic semper tyrannis!" Then, with a rapid stage stride, he crossed the stage, and disappeared from view. A piercing shriek from the President's box, a repeated call for "Water! water!" and "A surgeon!" in quick succession, conveyed the truth to the almost paralyzed audience. A most terrible scene of excitement followed. With loud shouts of "Kill him!" "Lynch him!" part of the audience stampeded toward the entrance and some to the stage.

I leaped from the top of the orchestra railing in front of me upon the stage, and, announcing myself as an army surgeon, was immediately lifted up to the President's box by several gentlemen who had collected beneath. I happened to be in uniform, having passed the entire day in attending to my duties at the Signal Camp of Instruction in Georgetown, and not having had an opportunity to change my dress. The cape of a military overcoat fastened around my neck became detached in clambering into the box, and fell upon the stage. It was taken to police head-quarters, together with the assassin's cap, spur, and derringer, which had also been picked up, under the supposition that it belonged to him. It was recovered weeks afterward, with much difficulty.

When I entered the box, the President was lying upon the floor surrounded by his wailing wife and several gentlemen who had entered from the private stairway and dress-circle. Assistant Surgeon Charles A. Leale, U.S.V., was in the box, and had caused the coat and waist-coat to be cut off in searching for the wound. Dr. A.F.A. King of Washington was also present, and assisted in the examination. The carriage had been ordered to remove the President to the White House, but the surgeons countermanded the order, and he was removed to a bed in a house opposite the theater. The wound in the head had been found before leaving the box, but at that time there was no blood oozing from it. When the dying President was laid upon the bed in a small but neatly furnished room opposite the theater, it was found necessary to arrange his great length diagonally upon it.

The room having become speedily filled to suffocation, the officer in command of the provost guard at the theater was directed to clear it of all except the surgeons. This officer guarded the door until relieved later in the evening by General M.C. Meigs, who took charge of it the rest of the night, by direction of Mr. Stanton.

A hospital steward from Lincoln Hospital did efficient service in speedily procuring the stimulants and sinapisms ordered.

The wound was then examined. A tablespoonful of diluted brandy was placed between the President's lips, but it was swallowed with much difficulty. The respiration now became labored; pulse 44, feeble; the left pupil much contracted, the right widely dilated; total insensibility to light in both. Mr. Lincoln was divested of all clothing, and mustard-plasters were placed on every inch of the anterior surface of the body from the neck to the toes. At this time the President's eyes were closed, and the lids and surrounding parts so injected with blood as to present the appearance of having been bruised. He was totally unconscious, and was breathing regularly but heavily, an occasional sigh escaping with the breath. There was scarcely a dry eye in the room, and it was the saddest and most pathetic death-bed scene I ever witnessed. Captain Robert Lincoln, of General Grant's staff, entered the room and stood at the headboard, leaning over his dying father. At first his terrible grief overpowered him, but, soon recovering himself, he leaned his head on the shoulder of Senator Charles Sumner, and remained in silent grief during the long, terrible night.

About twenty-five minutes after the President was laid upon the bed, Surgeon-General Barnes and Dr. Robert King Stone, the family physician, arrived and took charge of the case. It was owing to Dr. Leale's quick judgment in instantly placing the almost moribund President in a recumbent position the moment he saw him in the box, that Mr. Lincoln did not expire in the theater within ten minutes from fatal syncope. At Dr. Stone's suggestion, I placed another teaspoonful of diluted brandy between the President's lips, to determine whether it could be swallowed; but as it was not, no further attempt was made.

Some difference of opinion existed as to the exact position of the ball, but the autopsy confirmed the correctness of the diagnosis upon first exploration. No further attempt was made to explore the wound. The injury was pronounced mortal. After the cessation of the bleeding, the respiration was stertorous up to the last breath, which was drawn at twenty-one minutes and fifty-five seconds past seven; the heart did not cease to beat until twenty-two minutes and ten seconds after seven. My hand was upon the President's heart, and my eye on the watch of the surgeon-general, who was standing by my side, with his finger upon the carotid. The respiration during the last thirty minutes was characterized by occasional intermissions; no respiration being made for nearly a minute, but by a convulsive effort air would gain admission to the lungs, when regular, though stertorous, respiration would go on for some seconds, followed by another period of perfect repose. The cabinet ministers and others were surrounding the death-bed, watching with suspended breath the last feeble inspiration; and as the unbroken quiet would seem to prove that life had fled, they would turn their eyes to their watches; then, as the struggling life within would force another fluttering respiration, they would heave deep sighs of relief, and fix their eyes once more upon the face of their dying chief.

The vitality exhibited by Mr. Lincoln was remarkable. It was the opinion of the surgeons in attendance that most patients would have died within two hours from the reception of such an injury; yet Mr. Lincoln lingered from 10:30 p.m. until 7:22 a.m.

This small excerpt of Taft's diary, on display at the library, has captured the last hours of Abraham Lincoln in significant detail, but it is, believe it or not, far from the most macabre item in the collection.

That honour belongs to a piece of cloth, no larger than the size of a business card, that is stained with Lincoln's blood. (The towel it was cut from was placed under the President's head after he was shot.)

This has led many to speculate on whether an item so closely tied to the president's assassination (and perhaps also the many artifacts that brilliantly document the man's legacy) might inspire Lincoln's spirit to visit the library. Does he, perhaps, sit among the items and reflect on his life and those last fateful moments as the haunted echoes of a gunshot reverberates through the stacks?

Then there's the assassin, John Wilkes Booth, who himself had a morbid link to Montreal. Booth made regular visits to Montreal prior to the incident and had planned, after murdering the president, to flee to Canada in order to seek political refuge. Booth never made it to Canada — he was shot in the neck by Sergeant Boston Corbett inside a tobacco barn that had been set on fire in Virginia and died several hours later. One of the items found on Booth's body was a bank receipt from Montreal's Ontario Bank, dated October 27, 1864. (The Ontario Bank was acquired by the Bank of Montreal in 1906.)

*　*　*

If, after spending time with the ephemera of Lincoln's life and death and, perhaps, his spirit, you ascend two more staircases, you may encounter an eerie old man who, when addressed, turns to stare at you before vanishing into thin air.

According to a blog post on the Haunted Montreal website, the sixth floor of the McLennan library is haunted by an elderly man in an old-fashioned coat. People who have encountered the old man claim to have seen him floating above the floor or gliding up quietly behind an unsuspecting victim. There he lurks, staring intently at them until he is noticed. After the man's target has leapt from their seat, startled, and perhaps let out a scream of terror, he immediately fades from view, leaving his chosen victim embarrassed and confused.

Research conducted by the Haunted Montreal group into the potential source of this mysterious old man uncovered the nineteenth-century tale of a beautiful home that stood on the same grounds as the library and the bachelor named Jesse Joseph who lived there.

Joseph, who died in 1904 at the age of eighty-six, is said to have rolled over in his grave when his beautiful home and the magnificent gardens he used to take such pride in tending to were used as a headquarters for the McGill chapter of the Canadian Officer Training Corps. Later, in 1955, the house was demolished due to structural issues. An empty lot overrun with weeds stood for a dozen years where his gardens once flourished.

Haunted Montreal also uncovered a photo of Jesse Joseph wearing an old coat that seems to match the eyewitness accounts of the "strange, old coat" that the spectre on the library's sixth floor wears.

These eerie and morbid experiences dispute the claim made by many that a library is a boring and uninteresting place. If anyone tries to tell you this, you can share what you now know about the fascinating and decidedly hair-raising collection found in McGill's library.

Cholera Ghosts and Un-Ghosts
St. Antoine Cemetery/Dorchester Square

C holera came to Montreal on a ship called *Voyageur*.
It docked in June 1832, and as the passengers disembarked one man was left behind, lying on the deck, his body twitching in agony. The health commissioner was quickly called in and it didn't take long for him to make his diagnosis: cholera. Unfortunately, the man on the deck was not the only person on the ship who had been infected. Other passengers, who had already disembarked, were also carrying the deadly virus, and soon the highly contagious disease spread through the city like wildfire.

Within days Montreal was transformed. Barrels of burning tar sat on street corners to purify the air. Gravediggers travelled the roads to collect the bodies in their "dead-carts," crying out, "Have you any dead?" People were dropping like flies.

At the time, the lovely park we now know as Dorchester Square was actually a graveyard called St. Antoine Cemetery. The road leading up to it (now Cathedral Street) was called Cemetery Street, because it was the lane the dead-carts rode up from Saint Antoine Street in the Old Port to deposit the corpses at the cemetery. Within three days of the outbreak, there were 150 coffins stacked in the cemetery awaiting burial. That was only the beginning, though.

Over a thousand people died in June alone. Although the health commissioner insisted that every corpse be buried within six hours of death in order to stop the spread of the disease, the gravediggers simply couldn't keep up. The Sulpician priests came in to help with the digging. As it was simply impossible to dig separate graves for each body, they instead dug long trenches that were eight feet deep, ten feet wide, and one hundred feet long. The crude coffins were stacked inside these trenches with no indication of name. They were the anonymous dead.

In the 1830s cholera was still very much a mystery to medical professionals. As recounted by Donovan King on his downtown Montreal ghost walk, doctors would treat the disease with a variety of methods, including bleeding, leeches, bed rest, and even opium. We know now that opium can slow a person's breathing and heart so significantly that they appear dead, when in fact they aren't. But such details, as well as knowledge of the proper dosages of the drug, weren't readily available in the early nineteenth century. As a result, there were some horrifying scares during this period: poor unfortunates, believed to be dead, would rise up and terrify everyone. It was as if the dead were rising from their graves! Of course, eventually it was established that they were never dead to begin with, but until then there was great public fear. So, on top of the all the dead bodies crowding St. Antoine Cemetery, the mourners, the bawling children, the dead-carts, and the digging priests, there was also a small rash of "un-ghosts" to deal with, crawling out of their graves and wondering why everyone was screaming at them.

Let's examine a few of these un-ghost's tales.

Bill Collins: Not Quite Buried

Though the impossibility of burying all the dead quickly was a huge crisis for the city on the whole, it was the one thing that saved Bill Collins.

When Bill died he was taken to the cemetery by one of the dead-carts. Since there were no open graves, Bill was left on the ground for the night. Bill, who had been suffering from cholera but had somehow fought off the disease, woke up sometime in the night, not at all dead, and started walking down Saint Antoine Street, bewildered. A police officer saw Bill coming toward him in his winding sheet and ran off in a panic, crying out that the dead were coming out of their graves!

The confusion was quickly dealt with and Bill went on to live to the ripe age of ninety-two.

Hervieux: Tried to Escape

There was a woman known only by the first name Hervieux who wasn't as lucky as Bill. She was visiting friends when she became ill quite suddenly. Fearing the worst, her hosts sent for a doctor, who medicated her with opium right away, then tried bleeding her and applying leeches. Sadly, Hervieux did not respond to these efforts, and she was pronounced dead the next morning. She was quickly buried in St. Antoine Cemetery in her dress and jewellery, and because she was more wealthy than some, she was given her own grave and a cross carved with her name marked the spot.

The cemetery was closed in 1854, and some, but not all, of the buried were moved to the newer Mount Royal Cemetery on the mountain. Some years thereafter, workers were digging a ditch when they came upon a coffin. It was disturbing. This coffin, later identified as Hervieux's, had been broken from the inside, and a woman's arm protruded from it. Poor Hervieux, drugged with opium, had not been dead when she was buried and had been unable to dig herself free.

Unknown: The Woman Who Didn't Die, but Later Did

The perished poor sometimes weren't even given the dignity of a rickety coffin, as was the case of a woman whose body was dumped in one of the long trenches after she was believed to have died. As recounted on a ghost walk of the Old Port conducted by Montreal Ghosts, she, like so many others, had been administered opium and was not actually dead. So there she was, in a trench full of corpses, when fifteen hours later she suddenly woke up. She managed to claw her way out of the trench and proceeded to walk home, completely naked and yelling for help. Her neighbours looked out their windows and saw the woman whose body they'd seen taken away on a death-cart the day before walking down their street. Is it surprising they thought she was a ghost?

Unfortunately, though she was an un-ghost that day, the unnamed woman did become a ghost one week later, when cholera finally took her life.

* * *

Dorchester Square is now a pleasant park visited often in the summer months by professionals on their lunch break. Little do they know that there are 70,000 corpses under their feet. With so many dead in one place, there are bound to be strange phenomena about. Over the years disembodied voices and mumbled prayers have been heard. Orbs have been spotted floating through the trees. Most disturbing of all, piercing screams have disturbed the nighttime quiet in the park more than once.

There is a stomach-turning explanation for those screams that dates back to the cholera epidemic. As so little was known about cholera, doctors were desperate for more information about the disease and started performing autopsies on fresh cadavers in order to get it. The dissection of corpses was still illegal in Canada at this time, but the medical community was desperate. They erected autopsy sheds in the cemetery, conveniently located right next to the corpses waiting for burial, and got to work.

People were scandalized by what they saw as desecration of the bodies of the dead, and the newspapers called the sheds slaughterhouses. Catholic residents turned to their priests to put an end to this practice and the clergy moved in, but for a far different reason.

Knowing that the unbaptized wouldn't be able to get into heaven, the city's priests became concerned about unborn babies dying of cholera in their mother's wombs. They devised a grisly solution. Thirty willing pregnant cholera sufferers lined up outside these autopsy sheds and entered, one by one. Inside, the doctors performed hasty C-sections on the dying women, after which the priests sprinkled the newborns with holy water, thus savings their souls before their untimely deaths. The screams of the mothers could be heard for kilometres … perhaps the very same screams reaching us now.…

Haunted Grounds:
Ghosts of Duggan House
McGill University

D uggan House is haunted.

Located on McTavish Street, the gothic mansion was built in 1861 as a family home for Orrin S. Wood, one of the pioneers of the telegraph industry in Canada and president of the Montreal Telegraph Company. The home passed through the hands of many prominent families over the years, owned at one time by Matthew Hamilton Gault, MP and founder of Sun Life Financial, as well as George Herrick Duggan, a prominent engineer who gave the property to McGill University after his death in 1946. It is still owned by McGill to this day.

The paranormal phenomena experienced in Duggan House is well-known to faculty and students. There's the story of the graduate student who saw a female ghost in nineteenth-century dress coming down the stairs while she was in a meeting with her professor in the foyer, an experience that horrified her so much that she hyperventilated. Others have heard footsteps echoing through the halls, and found objects mysteriously moved or missing. It's rumoured that the Faculty of Commerce vacated the building in 1977 because students were uncomfortable with the paranormal activity going on in the place.

So, who exactly is haunting Duggan House?

If you've already read the chapter "The Tobogganing Ghost of Simon McTavish," you might be surprised to learn that anyone would be silly

Duggan House, built in 1861, is now owned by McGill University.

enough to build on the land where McTavish's castle once stood, but that's exactly what happened. Duggan House sits on that land, and was actually built with stones from the demolished castle, leading some to suggest that it might be McTavish himself who is haunting the building. But then, McTavish isn't a woman....

Another creepy theory has to do with Purvis Hall, another McGill campus building. Apparently, in the 1940s, when students were either lazier or more sensitive to the cold, a tunnel was built to connect the Purvis and Duggan buildings so students could travel easily between the two. In itself, this fact is alarming enough. That tunnel, if it's still accessible, could be letting all kinds of riff-raff into Duggan House, and seems like a pretty serious security issue. But it gets better. Purvis Hall is also believed to be haunted — by its namesake, Arthur B. Purvis. So, possible murderers and thieves aside, the tunnel may also be in use by the ghost of Arthur B. Purvis, intent on haunting any building he can get into.

But the Purvis Hall ghost isn't female either, is he?

There is one woman who lived in Duggan House who is a likely candidate for the female ghost spotted by the graduate student. Elizabeth Joanna Bourne, wife of Matthew Hamilton Gault, birthed a total of sixteen children, five of whom died in infancy. When the last baby perished it's said the poor lady went somewhat mad. She passed away in 1908. Does she haunt the building still? Could be, but it's difficult to be sure. When you're on haunted grounds, there are just too many ghosts to choose from.

The Echo of Footsteps
Trafalgar Tower, Westmount

*H*ave *you heard the story about the strange old hermit who used to live in the ruins of Trafalgar Tower? Legend has it that his ghost, forever tied to the location of the now-lost structure, still creeps about the grounds there. If you listen carefully, you might still hear his footsteps echoing down the empty street ...*

These words, shared in whispers, are the type of story still told about a building that long ago ceased to be a part of the Montreal landscape. Of course, tales of an old hermit who lived in the abandoned tower are just one of the legends shared about this historical locale.

Trafalgar Tower was built after John Ogilvy, a British loyalist, purchased a large expanse of land where General Amherst's troops had camped in October of 1760 before taking Montreal from the French settlers. A hexagon-shaped Gothic-style structure, the stone tower was built by James Gillespie.

Shortly after Ogilvy's death in 1819, the tower began to wear away due to the weather, but that didn't stop a number of spectral beings from taking up residence there.

In 1880, a couple was visiting the tower one winter morning when the man peered curiously through one of the tower windows. No sooner had he lifted himself up to look inside than he heard the distinct sound of approaching footsteps. His wife, hearing them as well, suggested that he get down from the window lest he be called out for trespassing. As the sound of the footsteps grew closer, the man turned to greet the visitor. Not only was there nobody there, but the snow itself was completely undisturbed in the direction they had sworn the footsteps were coming from.

An archivist named Dr. Massicotte also claimed to have had a very similar experience in the winter of 1925. He heard the mysterious disembodied footsteps, but saw no one and also swore there was no evidence of footsteps in the surrounding snow.

A theory posited by Donovan King on Haunted Montreal about the mystery of the footsteps relates to the location of the tower on a perch in the valley. It is possible, he speculates, that the geography of the landscape would have produced an eerie echo that might explain the recurrence of the footsteps tale by visitors.

Whether or not that explains the sound of the footsteps, there are other incidents that are not so easy to explain. One involves an old tollgate keeper by the name of Quinn who followed one of his cows toward the tower after the beast had wandered off in the middle of a moonlit night. When Quinn arrived at the tower he spotted not only his cow, standing at the foot of the haunted summer house, but something that took his breath away: a vision of a beautiful woman standing in one of the windows and looking out.

"I was transfixed to the spot and could not take my eyes off the vision," Quinn said. "She was in white with her hands clasped, as if in prayer, looking upwards. I remember falling down on my knees and crossing myself, and I remember nothing more."

Who was this spectre? She could have been the ghost of one of the many who were buried in the Trafalgar Mount Cemetery, which was founded on sixteen acres of Ogilvy's farmland in 1848. The cemetery advertised Trafalgar Tower as a beautiful part of the landscape that would make a luxurious resting spot for the remainder of eternity. There are, after all, many interred there whose spirits may wander the ground.

King mentions another possible spectral inhabitant. Railroad engineer W.R. Casey, who died of tuberculosis in Trafalgar Cottage and whose body was buried near the ascent to Trafalgar Tower, under the shade of nearby trees, may have found peace there — or not. Could Casey be one of the ghosts who haunts those grounds? Could it be the ghost of the hermit from local lore? And who was the woman who appeared in the vision shared by gatekeeper Quinn?

* * *

Trafalgar House, built in 1848, still stands on Côte-des-Neiges Road. But the last evidence of the tower before it crumbled comes from a letter written in 1946, in which a Montreal schoolteacher by the name of Martha Brown mentions that one of her students took a snapshot of the remains of Trafalgar Tower in 1937. "As you pass from Côte-des-Neiges along the Boulevard," she writes, "Belvedere Ave. is on the right, and the Tower used to be easily seen on the elevation just above the Boulevard."

Local citizens continue to share tales of echoing of footsteps in the area. A teenage girl from the neighbourhood often heard the sound of invisible footsteps echoing down the deserted street in the early morning hours or near sunset.

Even though Trafalgar Tower no longer stands, the eerie tales surrounding it, as well as the accompanying mystery and unanswered questions that linger like echoing footsteps, continue to live on.

Clubbers Beware
1234 rue de la Montagne

I t's 2005 and Club 1234 on rue de la Montagne is packed. Her voice nearly drowned out by the music pounding through the building, a drunken party girl asks a waiter if she can go up to the attic.

"Absolutely not," he tells her. "The attic is off-limits."

Not to be deterred, the girl stumbles upstairs as soon as he turns his back. Only moments later, the clubbers below hear a terrible scream cut through the bass line. Seemingly in mortal terror, the girl dives through an attic window, landing on the lower balcony. Still screaming like the devil is after her, she launches herself right off the balcony and into the arms of the bouncers below.

"What happened?" they ask her. "What's wrong?" But the girl can't stop screaming long enough to tell them.

Someone calls 911 and an ambulance comes to take the hysterical party girl away, her screams mingling with the sounds of the sirens.

What this girl saw has never been discovered, but one thing is certain: 1234 rue de la Montagne is haunted. And the ghosts who live there will make you want to jump to your death. According to Donovan King of the Haunted Montreal blog, the building that currently houses Club Le Cinq in downtown Montreal has had a long and varied history. The house was originally built as a family dwelling in 1859. Though it was later owned by Sir Alexander Tilloch Galt, a famous Canadian politician, the most significant use of the dwelling began in 1902, when it was purchased by Joseph C. Wray and Bros. and transformed into a funeral home.

By the late 1970s, the Wray brothers had moved on and the building lay abandoned. It was eventually purchased and converted into a nightclub, though there was a lot of turnover through the decades. The spot has housed many different clubs, including Club L'Esprit, Club 1234, World Beat Complex, and the current Club Le Cinq. But no matter the name on the door, ghostly sightings and paranormal occurrences have remained steady.

In the 1980s, while the building was being renovated, construction workers spotted a white orb drifting through the air. Understandably alarmed, the workers complained to the owner, who either didn't believe them or didn't care. He would be taught a lesson later that same night.

Dropping by the site to see how the renovations were going, the owner noticed a beautiful woman standing by herself at the bar with her back to him. It seemed strange to him, since the club wasn't open yet. Planning to ask her what she was doing there, the owner took a seat next to the woman at the bar and asked her if she needed anything. When she turned to him, he nearly fell off his stool.

The woman had no face.

There was no gaping wound or skull peeking back at him, either. Instead, there was a blank plane of skin, as though her face had been surgically removed. Completely horrified, the owner bolted from the building, never to return. The renovations were never finished.

Certain locations in the building house more ghosts than others. The women's bathroom in the basement is one such place, so haunted that female patrons are often warned not to go down there without a buddy. Several times club-goers have reported seeing a ghostly woman in the bathroom with a jagged scar on full display that runs all the way down her torso. It's the kind of scar that might be left by a mortician's knife … when the building was a funeral home, the basement is where the autopsies were conducted.

Even a space as innocuous as the coatroom isn't safe, where a small table has been known to fling itself across the room without warning.

And then there's the infamous attic, where our poor party girl saw what she saw and flung herself from the window. Though the window in question has since been boarded up, there have been multiple reports of pedestrians down on the street glimpsing a woman's ghost in that window, perhaps the same ghost that frightened our friend out of her wits. Three staff members who crept up to the attic on a dare all reported seeing something floating by the wall.

Even the famous and their entourages aren't immune. During the disco craze, when the club was especially popular and attracted such celebrities as Mick Jagger and David Bowie, Boy George's bodyguard wandered upstairs looking for the star. Though he saw nothing out of the ordinary, he felt an unseen presence nearby that made all the hair on his body stand on end. It took nearly a week for the goosebumps to go away.

So well-known as a haunted site is 1234 rue de la Montagne that it's been visited by multiple paranormal investigators throughout the years. It was featured on the TV show *Creepy Canada* in 2004. On the episode, it was suggested that the corpses had been defiled during their stay at the funeral home and were not able to find their eternal rest … and it is these ghosts that haunt the building to this day.

Another investigation was done in 2010 for a French TV show called *Rencontres Paranormales*. The owner of the club at the time, popular Montreal DJ MC Mario, had witnessed several unexplained incidents on the premises. He reported that he heard doors slamming on their own and the voice of a young girl singing. A team of twelve investigators was brought in with their equipment to explore the club and search for ghosts. One picture was captured of what could possibly be the face of a female ghost.

The team also conducted a seance in which they contacted the spirit of Galt's first wife. She claimed to be annoyed with the club and its patrons because their noise and antics were bothering her daughter, another haunter of the building. In an amusing deal made during the seance, MC Mario agreed to play Mozart at the beginning of each evening to appease the ghosts, as long as they agreed to leave the living alone. Apparently, Mozart was played each evening as promised, until Club 1234 closed its doors in early 2013. No ghostly encounters have been reported since.

A Montrealer's Experience with Slade the Spiritualist

Montreal Star, 1881

Henry Slade (1835–1905) was a famous medium and spiritualist who lived and performed across North America and Europe. He was acclaimed, most notably, for the use of slate-writing. During the ritual, a small slate and a piece of chalk would be placed under the table, and the messages revealed on the slate after the seance was performed were allegedly written by the spirit that had been reached.

The following letter to the editor of the *Montreal Star* from a Montreal resident was uncovered by John Robert Colombo for his book *More True Canadian Ghost Stories*.

A Montrealer's Experience with Slade, the Spiritualist

To the Editor of the *Star*:

Sir — I notice that two or three of your correspondences have been discussing spiritualism in your columns of late. I took some interest in the discussion, as I have had some strange experience of spiritualists, and I do not know whether mediums are frauds or connecting links between man and the spirit land. But I will tell you what occurred to me in New York the other day.

I heard a good deal about Slade, the medium. He is said to be by far the best-known "slate-writing medium" in the world. Whether his power is due to hypnotic influences, or to what Dr. Hammond called "syggognicism," I do not know, but he certainly can perform some of the most remarkable things it has ever been my lot to witness. But I will tell you exactly all I saw.

I saw Slade at midday. The room was well furnished, and of course there was plenty of light. I was courteously received, and was then invited to take my seat at a walnut table. I asked permission to look under the table to see if there was any apparatus by which he could be assisted, and he replied "Certainly." I knocked on the table, turned it over and failed to see anything unusual.

Then I sat down and Slade sat opposite me. He took my hands and the raps commenced at once. He ordered them whenever he pleased and he was obeyed. I asked if he would allow me to put my foot on his and again he replied "Certainly," and with both his hands in mine and both his feet under my feet the raps continued the same as ever, I was satisfied. I could not discover how the raps were produced, and I believed that Slade could produce raps whenever he pleased without detection.

Then I asked for the slate trick. But on this point I may tell you that I had brought my own slate. I could not be satisfied by allowing Slade to use one of his. It might be merely rubbed over with some chemical compound that by turning towards the light might cause words or phrases to reappear. So I brought my own and am satisfied that Slade did not tamper with it. I had even provided the pencil and when I told Slade, he said "All right." I handed him the slate and he placed it on the table and I bent over and immediately heard a scratching sound inside. This continued for some time, when the slate was opened and the following message was written in a plain hand:

Why will people doubt when the fountain of wisdom is open and the truth of the new life made manifest to all. In a few years all will see the truths of which we know, and those who see them now are the heralds of the coming dawn.
  B. Franklin

I was puzzled. I did not believe that the spirit of "B. Franklin" had written these words, but I wondered if Slade had ever been under the influence of syggognicism or hypnotics? I did not think so, for I experienced no sensation such as people feel in recovering from the trance, I was the same then as I am now, writing this letter at home. But I must tell you more.

I asked Slade if he could give me a message from some well-known Canadian, and he replied, "I shall try." Once more the slate was closed, and soon after opened again, and the following letter, in a different handwriting, appeared on the slate:

There are principles and forces in nature unknown to science, and the ethics of spiritualism is their crowning glory.
  D'Arcy Mcgee

It will be seen that the spelling of McGee was wrong, and on pointing this out to Slade he said that he could not account for these things. Sometimes the spirits of the late illiterate made no mistakes, and sometimes the spirits of the late accomplished many.

But the marvellous was still before me. I saw a white hand and arm pull my trousers. A slate I held in my hand was jerked out of it, and passing under the table was then placed upon it. What could have done it? It was like shooting a rifle bullet around a corner. A hand patted me on the cheek. I saw it, felt it, but could not grasp it. There was no mistake unless indeed I was in a trance. The table was lifted until the four legs were six inches from the ground and with all my force I could not press it down. There was some force at work, but what it was I do not know, and when the performance was over, I left more bewildered than ever.

According to *Chambers Dictionary of the Unexplained*, slate-writing, which was a staple of many nineteenth-century mediums, was first employed and made popular by Henry Slade.

In 1876, John Nevil Maskelyne, a member of the Magic Circle and founder of the Occult Committee who was interested in exposing fraud and dispelling the notion of supernatural power, was called to testify against Slade in a London court.

As outlined in Tatiana Kontou's *The Ashgate Research Companion to Nineteenth-Century Spiritualism and the Occult*, Maskelyne, the author of the 1875 books *Modern Spiritualism* and *The Fraud of Theosophy*, was asked to reveal to the court how slate-writing could be performed without any spiritual assistance.

"There are slate-writing mediums such as Slade, who can use the toes for writing messages on slates laid on the floor under the table," writes David Phelps Abbott in the 1912 book *Behind the Scenes with the Mediums*. "The medium wears a shoe that he can slip off the foot easily, and the end of the stocking is cut away."

Even though Slade was exposed as a trickster, charged with fraud, and eventually disappeared from spiritualism circles, the inclusion of slate-writing in seances continues.

The Slave Who Burned a City:
The Trial of Marie-Joseph Angélique
Old Montreal

hile the debate between "innocent victim" or "fierce arsonist" continues to rage, like that once-spectacular fire in the spring of 1734, one thing is clear: The brutal torture and execution suffered by Marie-Joseph Angélique, who was convicted for this crime, also echoes hauntingly from history.

It was in the evening of April 10, 1734, when a startling cry of "Fire!" rang through the streets of Montreal.

Saint-Paul Street was ablaze. As the hospital and church bells rang out their warning, the wind coming in from the west helped the fire spread at an alarming rate. Within three hours, forty-six buildings were destroyed, including the Hôtel-Dieu of Montreal (a convent and hospital). The losses were spectacular. Hundreds of people, both wealthy and poor, suddenly found themselves homeless. Many lost everything they had.

It's not a surprise that the people of Montreal were quick to identify someone to blame.

That someone was a slave named Marie-Joseph Angélique.

Long before the disaster of the great fire in Old Montreal, Marie-Joseph Angélique's life was a tragic one. Born in Portugal in 1705, she was sold into slavery in her early teens. First purchased by a Flemish merchant named Nichus Block, she was eventually sent to North America, arriving in New England. It was there she was purchased by the French merchant François Poulin de Francheville, who brought her to Montreal to be a domestic slave in his home. The year was 1725, and Marie-Joseph was twenty years old.

Thérèse de Couagne, Francheville's wife, changed Marie-Joseph's name to Angélique, which was the name of her deceased daughter. Though this might seem like a touching tribute, there is nothing sentimental about slavery, and Marie-Joseph's life in the Francheville household was far from happy. Though unmarried, she had three children while living there, none of whom survived infancy. A slave named Jacques César, owned by a friend of the Francheville family, is believed to have been the father of the children. It's possible the two were forced to have sex in order to produce offspring.

The one ray of sunshine in Angélique's life was her lover, Claude Thibault, a white servant who also worked for the Franchevilles. The Montreal community of the time didn't approve of the relationship between a black slave and a white servant, which is hardly surprising. But given what we know of her personality, it's unlikely that she cared — for Angélique was hardly a meek and obedient slave. Instead, she is described as stubborn, willful, and bad-tempered, all of which would become more apparent as her hopes of one day winning her freedom began to slip from her grasp.

Francheville passed away in 1733. Sadly, his passing didn't mean freedom for Angélique, who was still owned by Francheville's widow, Thérèse de Couagne. Though freedom wasn't being offered, Angélique took the bold step of requesting her freedom from her mistress in December of 1733. She was denied. It's at this point that Angélique became furious and incredibly difficult to deal with. She argued constantly with the other servants and talked back to her mistress. She suddenly became obsessed with fire and she threatened to burn the other servants and kill her mistress, also by fire. Servants began to quit service in the Francheville household to get away from her. Angélique was a terror to behold.

Likely as a result of these alarming threats, Angélique was sold in 1734 to François-Étienne Cugnet for six hundred pounds of gunpowder. Cugnet planned to resell the girl in the West Indies. Furious that this was happening to her, and possibly thinking she had nothing left to lose, Angélique threatened to burn down her mistress's house with Madame de Couagne in it. Shortly thereafter, before she could be sent to Cugnet in Quebec City, Angélique made her first daring move: she ran away.

Her partner on the run was her lover, Thibault. Before running off, the two set fire to Angélique's bed, further solidifying the association with fire in the minds of the Francheville neighbours. They fled across the frozen St. Lawrence River, aiming for New England and the hope of a boat back to Portugal. Sadly, their escape didn't go as planned. Delayed by bad weather, they were caught in Chambly only two weeks after their initial escape and escorted back to Montreal. Angélique was returned to Madame de Couagne and Thibault was sent to jail. He would be released in April of 1734, just two days before the Montreal fire.

As the smoke cleared on the morning of April 11, rumours began to circulate that it was the slave Angélique and her lover who had set the blaze. The Canadian Mysteries website points to an Amerindian slave named Marie, *dite* Manon, as the originator of the rumour, as she claimed to have heard Angélique say she wanted to see her mistress burn. True or not, this rumour was enough for the king's prosecutor to order the arrest of both Angélique and Thibault. Angélique was apprehended quickly in the garden of the Hôtel-Dieu and taken to jail. Thibault, on the other hand, was never found and is believed to have fled. He was never seen again in New France.

Thus began the most spectacular trial of eighteenth-century Canada. Though trials in those days usually lasted only a couple of days, Angélique's would go on for six weeks. Charged with arson, she faced possible punishments of death, torture, or banishment if convicted. It's also important to keep in mind that in those days, the accused was presumed guilty and was expected to prove her own innocence. Lawyers were illegal. Twenty-nine-year-old Angélique had her work cut out for her.

More than twenty witnesses were called to the stand to testify against Angélique. None of them claimed to have seen Angélique set the fire, but they were all convinced she was the culprit. Surprisingly, Angélique's mistress Thérèse de Couagne was the only one to defend her, insisting her slave was innocent to the very end. But it was the testimony of a five-year-old girl that finally sealed Angélique's fate. Little Amable Lemoine Monière, a merchant's daughter, swore she had seen Angélique going up to the attic of the Francheville home with a shovel of live coals in her hand just before the fire started. It was all over.

Angélique's sentence was a horror in itself. Her hands would be cut off, and then she would be burned alive. Luckily (though is there really anything that can be deemed "lucky" in this story?) the sentence was appealed and lessened. Instead, Angélique was to be tortured, hanged, and her body burned. At this point, awaiting death in a Montreal prison, Angélique steadfastly maintained her innocence; not that it mattered. Torture was a commonplace punishment in this era, meant to illicit a confession. On June 21, 1734, Angélique was subjected to a method of torture called the Spanish boot, whereby the leg is crushed by planks of wood. Under this torture, Angélique eventually broke and admitted to setting the fire — though it should be noted that she never implicated Thibault.

They dressed her in a white chemise, had her hold a burning torch to symbolize her crime, and took her to Notre-Dame Basilica in a garbage cart. It was there that they hanged Marie-Joseph Angélique, displayed her body on a gibbet for two hours, then burned the corpse on a pyre.

Did Marie-Joseph Angélique set the fire that burned down Old Montreal in 1734? It's impossible to know for sure. Certainly the deck was stacked against her. As a black person, a woman, and a slave, it's unlikely she could ever have proven her innocence, no matter what she said or did. She was doomed from the moment of her arrest, there's no question. But an unjust system doesn't necessarily point to her innocence. Angélique certainly had an interest in arson. She hated her mistress. She yearned for her freedom. She very well might have set the fire.

Perhaps the better question is: does it matter? Her story is so much bigger than this one detail. It brings to the forefront Canada's participation in slavery, which is often overlooked. It's the story of an angry woman who was defiant to the last. It's the story of a love that was never betrayed. It's the story of a fight for freedom.

The square across from Montreal's city hall was renamed Place Marie-Joseph Angélique in 2012. It will ensure that her story will never be forgotten.

The Redpath Murders
The Redpath Mansion, Downtown Montreal

On June 13, 1901, two scandalous murders shook Montreal high society and a mystery that has yet to be solved was born. Two members of the Redpath family, one of Canada's wealthiest families at the time, lay dead with gunshot wounds to the head. The investigation into the murders was brief, police involvement spotty, and descriptions of the victims — their health and their states of mind, both before and on the day of the tragedy — were contradictory and confusing. The bodies were buried swiftly and very soon the murders were hardly spoken of, almost as though they'd never happened at all.

Questions surround this event: What happened in the Redpath Mansion on that fateful night? How could two such high-profile killings be left unsolved over a century later? And, most importantly, who shot Ada Maria Mills Redpath and Jocelyn Clifford Redpath, and why?

The story of the Redpath family begins with John Redpath, who immigrated to Montreal from Scotland in 1816. Working initially as a stonemason, Redpath quickly opened his own construction business, which was involved in the construction of the Lachine Canal, the Rideau Canal, and the Notre-Dame Basilica. Most notably, he established Canada's first sugar refinery, Canada Sugar Refining Company (now Redpath Sugar), in 1854. Though Redpath passed away in 1869, his extensive family (he had seventeen children) continued to enjoy the wealth amassed by his many successful business ventures, and by 1901 were firmly entrenched members of Montreal's elite.

John James Redpath was John Redpath's tenth child. He would grow up to work in his father's sugar refinery business, and in 1867 married Ada Maria Mills. He and Ada had five children: Amy, Peter, Reginald, Harold, and Jocelyn Clifford, known as "Cliff." It's here, in this branch of the Redpath family, that we find the major players in the Redpath mansion murders.

Ada Maria Mills and four of her five children.

Much of the minute-by-minute account of the murders on that day in the summer of 1901 can be found in the coroner's inquest documents, which includes testimony by Ada's son Peter. It is said that Cliff, aged twenty-four, returned home at about 6:00 p.m. on June 13 and went straight to his mother's room. Seconds later his brother Peter heard shots ring out.

After breaking down the door to the room, Peter found his mother and brother lying in pools of blood next to a revolver. According to a *Montreal Daily Star* article published the next day, Ada was already dying when Peter arrived but Cliff was rushed to Royal Victoria Hospital and died just before midnight.

There were no witnesses to the murders other than the victims themselves, and so it's impossible to know the most basic facts, such as who was shot first, who was holding the gun, what the two victims spoke about just before their deaths (if anything), and why one of them had a gun to begin with. Whether Ada or Cliff had a desire to die or to kill the other is also impossible to know, but we can speculate.

Reliable information about Ada Maria Mills Redpath isn't easy to come by. We know she was the daughter of John Easton Mills, who was elected mayor of Montreal in 1846 (and also shows up in the chapter "The Heroic Death of John Easton Mills"). We know that by 1901 she was the mother of five children and a widow (her husband, John James Redpath, died in 1884). We know that she was in poor health. And we know that she died after being shot in the head. Other details, even her exact age at the time of her death, are difficult to pin down. The Canadian Mysteries website states that Ada was born in 1842, which would make her fifty-nine at the time of her death. Other sources claim she was fifty-six, sixty-two, and forty-five, and one of those sources was her own child.

The exact nature of the ailments that plagued her is also difficult to ascertain, mainly due to the limits of medical knowledge in 1901. One source reports that she suffered from "ulceration of the eyes, neuralgia of the jaw, painful joints (which involved the fitting of a brace), and melancholia." After the murders, the *New York Times* stated that Ada "had been ill for some time, suffering greatly from insomnia." The *Globe* reports that Ada suffered from "partial paralysis of one side," though this isn't corroborated by any other sources. Most reports agree that today Ada would likely have been diagnosed with depression, though how severe it was is unclear. Canadian Mysteries claims she regularly spent time in a sanatorium and by 1900 hardly ever left her room. At the time of her death, Ada was in such poor health that she relied on her children to care for her. Of the five children, Amy and Clifford tended to her the most.

How sick and depressed was Ada? Depressed enough to take her own life? Reporters of the time seemed to think so. The *Halifax Morning Herald* reported in June 1901 that "while temporarily mentally deranged, Mrs. Redpath attempted to end her life, and in attempting to prevent her, the son was shot. The unfortunate lady then completed her undertaking." Similar stories came out in the *Calgary Herald* and the *Winnipeg Free Press*, and Manitoba's *Swan River Star* agreed with that description of events in an article that came out far later in the month.

But the coroner's inquest into Ada's death came to a different conclusion. The verdict was quite clear:

> Ada Maria Mills died at Montreal on the thirteenth day of June nineteen hundred & one, from a gunshot wound apparently inflicted by Clifford Jocelyn Redpath [the order of his names is written incorrectly in the report], while unconscious of what he was doing and temporarily insane, owing to an epileptic attack from which he was suffering at the time.

Is this true? It's time to turn to Jocelyn Clifford Redpath, Ada's youngest son. Having recently graduated with a degree in law from McGill, Cliff was studying to take the bar exam that summer. The *Montreal Daily Star* described Cliff as popular with his fellow students, ambitious, and interested in canoeing and horseback riding, all the traits of a picture-perfect young man of wealth. But outward appearances can be deceiving. Did Cliff's enviable exterior hide a distressing inner life?

Like his mother, Cliff was also said to have suffered from insomnia, according to the *Montreal Daily Star*. Dr. Roddick, the family's physician, who was called to the house on the night of the murders, had a lot more to say about Cliff, claiming he was epileptic, suffered from a neurological condition, was studying overly hard for his upcoming exam, and was stressed about having to care for this mother. Though he didn't for a moment suspect Cliff of violence, Dr. Roddick stated that, given his many burdens, he wasn't surprised the young man lost his mind.

Once the coroner's inquest declared Cliff to be the killer, the epilepsy explanation was printed in papers nationwide. As corroborated by a Dr. Rollo Campbell, who spotted foam in Cliff's mouth (evidence of an epileptic fit), this easy, tied-with-a-bow solution to the puzzling deaths seemed to satisfy some. In this version of the night, Cliff lost control during an epileptic seizure and shot both his mother and himself, though it's never quite clear if one — or both — of the shots was accidental.

Looking at this explanation today, some glaring issues become apparent. To begin with, epileptics are no longer assumed to be insane, and an epileptic seizure would never hold up in court as a reason for murder. Insomnia isn't known to drive anyone to murder either, though it's widely noted that both Ada and Cliff suffered from the affliction, as though this is somehow a motive. Studying too much is also a flimsy excuse for homicide.

Of course, Cliff might have accidentally shot a gun while having a seizure, but that doesn't explain what he was doing holding the gun to begin with. However, the press was keen to solve this mystery. Both the *Grandview Exponent* and the *Quebec Daily Mercury* reported that Cliff had been drinking on the day of the murders and that during a quarrel with his mother he shot both her and himself. *La Presse* insisted Cliff was deeply depressed. Cliff's brother Peter, whose story seemed to change drastically each time he was interviewed, eventually claimed that his brother was homosexual and he'd told his mother for the first time that day. This led to their argument and the subsequent shooting.

But each of these stories has its holes. In a contemporary article about the murders, Jeannette Novakovich claims Cliff's bar exam date was only a month away, and he'd already paid the fee, evidence that she believes shows he wasn't depressed or suicidal as other sources claim. There are no other reports of Cliff being gay. And returning to the epilepsy explanation, Novakovich points out that Cliff is never once stated to suffer from the condition in the many Redpath family diaries, not even once.

Mother kills son and then herself, or son kills mother and then himself. Neither explanation is particularly convincing, and so many questions remain, the main one being *why?* With that question in mind, we must turn at last to the strange events that took place after the bodies were discovered.

To begin with, no one called the police. The *Calgary Herald* reports that the police only heard of the murders by accident. The coroner's inquest states that three doctors were called instead. They confirmed Ada's death and came forth with the suspicion of an epileptic fit. Another strange thing to note is the extreme swiftness of the inquest and the burials, both of which were complete by June 15, just two days after the murders. There is little to no evidence that any investigation into the murders was conducted by the police beyond that day.

Novakovich explains that the Victorian obsession with keeping up appearances and sweeping unpleasantness under the rug could explain why the deaths were dealt with so quickly and hardly spoken of thereafter. If she's right, the Redpath murders could be a simple case of accidental death that nobody wanted to talk about, a mystery that lived on mainly due to our overactive imaginations. Or maybe not.

Maybe the Redpaths had a killer in their midst, and didn't want anyone to find out. Maybe Ada wasn't an invalid but was hidden away due to her alarming tendency to pull out a revolver without warning and shoot off a couple of rounds. Maybe Cliff really was an angry drunk set on killing his mother. Or maybe the murderer was someone else entirely. After all, there was an entire mansion full of rooms to hide in that night, rooms that, it seems, nobody searched. Rooms the Redpath mansion murderer might have retreated into, slipping deep into the shadows and out of sight forever.

The Heroic Death of John Easton Mills
The Wellington Basin

Although it isn't widely known, John Easton Mills, who served as mayor of Montreal from 1846 to 1847 — for less than a year — has a ghostly connection. He was sworn in as mayor in December 1846 and had barely settled into his office when he was faced with a major crisis. In the spring of 1847, the Irish potato famine caused thousands of Irish immigrants to flee to North America. Many ended up in Montreal, and before the year was out, 6,000 Irish, weak from hunger and disease-ridden, would die on the shores of the city. Many local inhabitants, including the new mayor, died too, victims of the diseases brought by the newcomers. The death toll was enormous, so it's hardly surprising that there are a lot of ghosts from those days.

The Irish potato famine, also called the Great Famine, was caused by a potato blight that was felt all over Europe. Over three million Irish people were entirely dependent on the potato for food, so when at least one-third of the potato crop in the country was lost to blight in 1845 it was a disaster. In 1846 three-quarters of the crop was lost. The people were starving. One million Irish people would die over the course of the famine, which lasted from 1845 to 1849. During that same time, a million Irish chose to emigrate to save themselves. The destination for one hundred thousand of those immigrants? Canada.

In her *Montreal Gazette* article "Montreal, Refugees and the Irish Famine of 1847," Marian Scott states that of those one hundred thousand, seventy thousand Irish immigrants arrived in Montreal, which had a population of only fifty thousand at the time. They made the three-month journey to the New World on ships that were used to carry lumber to Europe. Normally the ships were weighed down with rocks for the journey home to make up for the weight of the wood, but as so many people were desperate to make the journey, human beings were used to fill the ships instead. These ships weren't meant to transport people, and conditions on board were horrific. The boats were crowded and violence abounded. There was no system to get rid of human waste. Disease was everywhere, especially typhus, which was spread by lice. Death by typhus is hardly pleasant; symptoms including shivering, aches, bloating of the face, muscular twitching, delirium, a darkening of the skin, and a rapidly spreading rash. The bodies of those who died during the journey, which numbered in the thousands, were simply thrown overboard.

When these "coffin ships" arrived in the Wellington Basin, Montrealers were aghast. A great number of the travellers died right there on the wharfs. A medical superintendent of the time said that the odour wafting from the immigrant ships was like the stink of a dunghill.

The influx of the sick onto the island horrified the population, who were terrified that typhus would spread across the city. Their fears weren't baseless — the mortality rate for untreated typhus is up to 60 percent. As a result, the immigrants were kept on the waterfront, housed in fever sheds that spread across the shore, filled to bursting with the sick and dying.

Mayor John Easton Mills felt compassion for the suffering Irish. Bruce Davis reports in a *Montreal Gazette* article that Mills welcomed the immigrants, despite the protests of Montrealers, and supervised the construction of more sheds, outhouses, hospital wards, and surgical rooms. He assured citizens that the sick were being kept at the waterfront, and they had nothing to fear.

Public outrage at the situation flared, however, when a young immigrant girl was spotted on the corner of Notre-Dame and McGill Streets begging for change. An angry mob marched to city hall, calling on the mayor to fix this problem or prepare to face vigilante justice. They went

The Irish Commemorative Stone, also known as the Big Black Rock, honours the thousands of Irish people who perished during their immigration to Canada.

so far as to threaten to throw the fever sheds and their inhabitants into the river. To appease the people, Mills ordered a wall be built around the basin with guards to monitor anyone coming or going.

The Church also did its part to help the sick. It's reported that the Mother Superior of the Grey Nuns said to the sisters in the convent: "I wish to send you to Wellington Basin [to help the typhus victims], but in doing so I am signing your death warrant. So if any of you don't wish to volunteer for this job, I will not hold it against you." All the sisters agreed to go to the waterfront to aid the sick. Seven of them would die. They were replaced by the sisters of Providence, who in turn were replaced by the sisters of the Hôtel-Dieu. Dozens and dozens of nuns and priests would perish after tending to the sick in the fever sheds. They were buried, along with the Irish, in trenches right next to the sheds themselves, the coffins piled three deep.

In the fall of 1847, the people of Montreal began to notice that the mayor had not been seen about town or made any public declarations of late. In fact, no one had seen his face in weeks. It wasn't long before it was revealed that the mayor had died of typhus, proving that status is no barrier against disease.

What the people didn't know at the time was that Mayor John Easton Mills had been sneaking down to the Wellington Basin on the sly and tending to the sick himself. It was there that he contracted the disease that eventually led to his death.

Today, if you're walking along the Lachine Canal, approaching the Wellington Basin, keep an eye out for a footbridge where many people report feeling uneasy. You may spot a number of white orbs floating above the bridge. You might also spot something even more remarkable: a ghostly man, quite tall, wearing a top hat. Some believe this spectre is the ghost of John Easton Mills. Though the clergy declared that Mills was assured a place in heaven due to his good works, the former mayor continues to pace the shores of his city, keeping watch over the long-gone fever sheds and the poor souls he couldn't save all those years ago.

The Pervasive Legend of the Flying Canoe: Honoré Beaugrand's Tale of a Deal with the Devil

There have been many stories about the terrible repercussions that befall those who make a deal with the Devil. The most popular French-Canadian version of the tale is perhaps the one that Honoré Beaugrand published in *Century Magazine* in August 1982 titled "La Chasse-Galerie."

Beaugrand, who was born in Saint-Joseph-de-Lanoraie, Quebec, in March 1848, joined the military and lived in Mexico and the United States before returning to his home province and settling in Montreal in 1878. He founded the daily Montreal newspaper *La Patrie* the following year. Beaugrand was known as a political reporter and writer. He eventually entered politics, too, serving as the mayor of Montreal between 1885 and 1886. Today there is a metro station named after him.

Despite his many other accomplishments, Beaugrand is most popularly known as the folklorist who told the tale of "La Chasse-Galerie" (which translates as "The Flying Canoe" or "The Bewitched Canoe"). In the story, a group of Gatineau loggers working at a remote lumber camp get to drinking heavily on New Year's Eve. Although they are enjoying the refreshments, they long to visit the sweethearts they left back home more than three hundred miles away.

To make such a journey in one night was impossible by conventional methods, so they make a pact with the Devil that enables their canoe to quickly fly through the air. As part of the pact they agree not to use the name of God, not to drink any liquor on the journey, to return before six o'clock the following morning, and not to touch any of the crosses on the church steeples they might fly over.

"Satan, king of the infernal regions," the men chant in unison, "we promise to sell our souls if within the following six hours we pronounce *le nom du bon Dieu*, your master and ours, or if we touch a cross on the voyage. On that condition you will transport us through the air, wherever we may want to go, and bring us back sound and safe to the shanty."

The men arrive at their desired location, enjoy the festivities and dance with their beloved sweethearts, and then set back on their journey home. Only Baptiste Durand, the group's navigator (who claims to have taken similar trips multiple times before), drank during the festivities. During the trip back, he swears, using the Lord's name in vain. The others overpower him and take over navigation of the canoe, which results in a harrowing near-death adventure before they return.

There are multiple variations of the original tale. Some have the men, who end up violating the conditions, condemned to fly the canoe through Hell itself, appearing every New Year's Eve. Another has the Devil himself steering the canoe, with the men managing to toss him overboard in order to escape.

Beaugrand's tale concludes with a wry statement:

> All I can say, my friends, is that it is not so amusing as some people might think, to travel in mid-air, in the dead of winter, under the guidance of Beelzebub, running *la chasse-galerie*, and especially if you have *un ivrogne* to steer your bark canoe. Take my advice, and don't listen to anyone who would try to rope you in for such a trip. Wait until summer before you go to see your sweethearts, for it is better to run all the rapids of the Ottawa and the St. Lawrence on a raft, than to travel in partnership with *le diable* himself.

Versions of The Flying Canoe *painting have been adapted regularly in Montreal, throughout Quebec, and across Canada.*

The Flying Canoe is a visual image that has been used continually in Quebecois and wider Canadian popular culture. La Ronde, Quebec's largest amusement park that was originally built for Montreal's Expo 67 (the 1967 World's Fair), had a ride that ran from the opening of the park until the spring of 2017 called La Pitoune. This ride, a log flume ride, used the legend of the flying canoe in its implementation, with an image of the Devil perched behind a group of terrified men and the high bench at the back of each log-car known as "the devil-seat."

The Montreal folk-metal band Blackguard used the image of a flying canoe on the cover of their second album, *Profugus Mortis*. The final track on this album, titled "The Last We Wage" is inspired by the Flying Canoe legend.

The name and label for "Maudite," a Belgian-style strong dark ale produced by Unibroue in Chambly, Quebec, less than an hour's drive from Montreal, also takes its inspiration from the legend. Maudite, which translates into English as "accursed" or "damned" was first released in

1992 and, with an alcohol content of 8 percent, was the first truly strong beer brewed in Canada.

As part of the opening ceremony for the Vancouver 2010 Winter Olympics, fiddler Colin Maier was lowered from the ceiling in a flying canoe, a direct allusion to the folktale.

In 1991 a series of Canadian folklore stamps issued a forty-cent postage stamp titled "Witched Canoe" in honour of this legend.

Perhaps now, when you see the ever-pervasive flying canoe motif in either Quebec or Canadian pop culture, you'll be able to nod knowingly, fully understanding the Montreal-based source of the legend.

Now for a Dow Debacle:
The Curse of the Old Dow Brewery
Griffintown

An old building, mostly abandoned since 1998 and contaminated with asbestos and an apparent curse, stands empty, haunting the Griffintown neighbourhood with memories of a once-brighter time of prosperity and growth … if it hadn't been for a serious of unfortunate events that altered its fate.

The Molson Brewery, founded in 1786, is not only Canada's oldest brewery but the oldest in North America. The brewery and its founder, John Molson, are known as a major Montreal success story. The family was involved in the creation of a bank (Molson Bank), which later merged into the Bank of Montreal, and diverse other investments, including the ownership of an NHL hockey franchise (the Montreal Canadiens), as well as shipping, railway, and lumber companies. They used their wealth to support the Montreal General Hospital and McGill College (now a university).

Though Labatt is often seen as Molson's main competitor for the Canadian beer market, there was another player, founded in the same city, which was Molson's main competitor and, at one time, Montreal's number one brewery. In fact, it might very well have sat strong among Canada's major long-standing breweries such as Molson, Labatt, Moosehead, and Alexander Keith's if not for the brand-shattering tragic events that occurred in the late 1960s.

Thomas Dunn started his brewing operations just a few years after John Molson in the town of La Prairie, across the St. Lawrence River from Montreal. He moved his growing operation to Montreal in the latter half of the first decade of the 1800s. The ownership of the company was assumed in 1834 by William Dow, who had risen in the ranks from employee, to foreman, and finally a partner in the company.

Dow Breweries went on to possess more than sixty plants and office buildings across the country, employing more than one thousand people. It was behind the construction of Canada's first and oldest planetarium (originally known as the Dow Planetarium, later named the Montreal Planetarium and currently the Rio Tinto Alcan Planetarium). As Allen Winn Sneath writes in his book *Brewed in Canada: The Untold Story of Canada's 350-Year-Old Brewing Industry*, by 1966, Dow Ale, the brewery's most popular beer, was the number-one selling brand in the province of Quebec.

Memorable advertising slogans such as "Now for a Dow," "Wouldn't a Dow go good now" and "Take Dow home" were well-known and the company's four most popular brands at the time were Dow Ale, Kingsbeer Lager, Champlain Porter, and Dow Porter.

Trouble began for the company when, in late 1965 and early 1966, nearly fifty men in Quebec City were hospitalized with a degenerative heart ailment. In a CBC television interview, Quebec's deputy minister of health, Jacques Gélinas, explained that the first death was reported in November of 1965, and by the middle of March 1966, another fifteen of those men had died. The deaths, he reported, occurred between twenty-four and forty-eight hours after the beginning of the illness. It was determined that one of the common factors found among the group were that the men were large consumers of beer, none of them drinking less than eight quarts of beer a day.

Because of the popularity of both Dow Ale and Champlain Porter in Quebec City at the time, and indications of a preference for Dow brewery beers in the surviving patients who were questioned, investigations into the brewing process began.

Despite the fact that, after a three-month investigation, no link was established between the heart trouble experienced and any of Dow

MILLION GALLONS

Down The Drain For Quebec Beer

No Definite Link Between 16 Deaths And Beer

But Dow Brewery Orders Entire Stock Dumped

QUEBEC (CP) — One million gallons of beer — Dow ale and Champlain porter brands — will be dumped into this city's sewage system within the next two to three weeks.

The move, announced in a statement in Montreal Wednesday by Dow Brewery Ltd., follows the deaths of 16 middle-aged Quebec-area men from cardiac troubles.

Although all 16 were said to have consumed large quantities of beer, a three-pronged investigation of the deaths has established no connection between the heart trouble and Dow beer,

Public relations debacle: Despite the fact that no link was established between the heart trouble experienced and any of Dow's beers, the company decided upon a public relations good faith campaign that backfired.

brewery's products, the company decided upon a good-faith campaign in order to help alleviate the concerns and rumours that surfaced.

In an April 3, 1966, interview with CBC television, Pierre Gendron, president of Dow Brewery, explained quite emphatically that after a thorough analysis of the beers nothing whatsoever was found. "There has been a tremendous amount of rumours and the population was very unnerved and very distressed about this and very nervous," Gendron noted, explaining that, even though the beer was perfectly good, as a responsible company they had no other choice than to recall it. "Now, if you take back a huge quantity of beer like this," he said, "there's no other choice, also, to dump it."

A *Winnipeg Free Press* article from March 1966 reported that one million gallons of Dow Ale and Champlain Porter brands of beer (comprising six hundred thousand gallons of stock at Dow's Quebec brewery and another four hundred thousand gallons from the brewer's agents, retail locations, and the public) would be dumped into sewers.

Instead of assuring the public, this stunt by Dow Breweries had the exact opposite effect. The public saw it as an admission of guilt, and in less than a year Dow lost its dominant position, its market share transferred to Molson and Labatt.

Within that year, a Canadian Medical Association article by Yves Morin and Phillippe Daniel found similarities between the Quebec case and other "beer poisoning" incidents, including ones that occurred in Omaha, Nebraska, and Manchester, England, in 1900. This study determined that the Quebec City brewery beers contained ten times more cobalt sulphate than the Montreal location. Cobalt sulphate is a chemical that had been added to some Canadian beers since 1965 in order to improve stability of the beer's head. The report indicated that in both Quebec City and in Omaha the syndrome began appearing a month after the introduction of cobalt sulphate to the beer and that no new cases occurred a month after the use of colbalt sulphate was discontinued.

Even though Dow Breweries stopped using cobalt sulphate in their beer and no new cases of the heart ailment were reported, the damage had been done. Dow never recovered from the 1966 debacle, and not long after the brewery was acquired by Molson. By 1998 both the production of Dow beer and the historic brewery on Notre-Dame Street were shut down.

* * *

Over the years the abandoned Dow Brewery building, originally erected in 1816, has attracted plenty of urban explorers, those interested in history, and, as often happens in old empty buildings, paranormal investigators.

In 1966, Dow Ale was the top-selling brand of beer in Quebec. Nobody foresaw the dark turn the company's fortunes would take.

The Montreal Paranormal Investigations group explains that the site is haunted by many ghosts, including that of a young girl who was murdered near the location in the late 1990s. Outlining experiences of group member Patrick, as well as other psychics who didn't want to stay in the building because they felt that "death was under the ground," the group's website shared a visual phenomenon that Patrick had seen.

After he continually experienced "horrific ghost vibes" from the location and then identified the spot where the girl was allegedly murdered, Patrick caught a vision of the outline of a little girl, lit in the darkness. She had been crying, he explained. He went on to say that her tears were happy tears because she knew they were there to help her.

The Dow Brewery remains one of the staple locales of the historic tour of Haunted Griffintown. In keeping with the neighbourhood's brewing roots, once one finishes the ninety-minute tour, it might just be appropriate to end the evening at brewpub Brasseur du Montreal and offer a toast to the past with their aptly named Ghosttown porter.

Unspeakable Torture and Mind Control: Project MK-ULTRA

The Allan Memorial Institute, McGill University

T he term *unspeakable torture* is likely to conjure up images of a secret medieval underground dungeon echoing with the screams of prisoners strapped to a torture rack, the atrocities and experimentation performed on men, women, and children in a Nazi concentration camp, or perhaps a private Dr. Frankenstein–style lab in which a mad scientist secretly works away after midnight, performing unimaginable operations on the human body.

But scenes like this aren't only relegated to faraway places or to the imagination of science fiction and horror writers. Terribly similar events have taken place in the heart of Montreal ... and in the not-too-distant past.

The *Canadian Oxford Dictionary* describes *torture* as "the infliction of severe bodily pain, especially as a punishment or a means of interrogation or intimidation; severe physical or mental suffering." Coercion and mind control were at the centre of a controversial series of experiments that took place between 1957 and 1964 at the Allan Memorial Institute at McGill's Royal Victoria Hospital, partially funded by the CIA. They were inspired by a phenomenon observed in American soldiers who had been captured during the Korean War and whose behaviour was significantly and frighteningly altered.

Ravenscrag

These experimental atrocities couldn't have occurred in a more fitting building: an eerie, imposing, and intimidating Italian Renaissance–style mansion that clung to the foothills of Mount Royal. The building simply looks intimidating, and its original name was decidedly creepy and Poe-esque: Ravenscrag.

Built between 1860 and 1863 by Scottish-Canadian financier and shipping magnate Sir Hugh Allan on the fourteen acres he purchased at what was then considered the outskirts of the city, the mansion consisted of five floors and seventy-two rooms. The looming building was considered to be larger and more costly than any other building in Canada at the time, including the formidable Dundurn Castle in Hamilton, Ontario, constructed by Sir Allan Napier McNab thirty years earlier.

Like McNab, Allan, who died in 1882 as one of the wealthiest men in Canada, intended his property to be an impressive display of his prosperity and importance. During his tenure there, Allan could sometimes be seen looking down from the mansion's seventy-five-foot tower at the three-hundred-foot front yard, past the gate, and over Old Montreal.

Ravenscrag. The mansion was originally built in the early 1860s by the wealthy industrialist Hugh Allan. Following his death the building was bequeathed to McGill University and became the home of the Allan Memorial Institute.

In 1940, Sir Hugh Allan's son, Sir Montague Allan, donated the mansion to the Royal Victoria Hospital. The Allan Memorial Institute opened in July of 1944 and launched what was considered a very modern Department of Psychiatry as part of McGill University's Faculty of Medicine, with an initial offering of fifty-two patient beds.

MK-ULTRA

At the end of the Korean War, something was alarming the U.S. government. Some of the American soldiers who had been taken as prisoners of war returned home with decidedly different views, values, and thoughts, described as anti-American and Communist. U.S. government agencies, such as the CIA, believed this was evidence that foreign militaries had mastered methods of brainwashing and mind control as a powerful new weapon.

Fears that countries deemed hostile to the United States had the ability to use chemical and biological agents against Americans and their allies led to the development of a defence program designed to discover similar techniques. The plan was to develop these techniques so that American intelligence agents could learn to detect them and be able to counteract.

Among other efforts, such as Project CHATTER (a Navy project involving a "truth drug"), Project BLUEBIRD/ARTICHOKE (a program designed to promote memory enhancement and the establishment of defensive means for preventing hostile mind control), and MKNAOMI (a covert support base to meet clandestine operational requirements and stockpile severely incapacitating and even lethal materials), MK-ULTRA was developed.

MK-ULTRA, approved by the director of Central Intelligence on April 13, 1953, was the principal CIA program concerned with the research and development of chemical, biological, and radiological agents capable of employment in clandestine operations to control human behaviour.

MK-ULTRA documents were destroyed in 1973 under the orders of Dr. Sidney Gottlieb, Chief of Technical Services Division. But various hearings, pieces of testimony, and recorded eyewitness accounts survived and can be put together to create a disturbing and unforgettable tale. In an almost 180-page document of a United States Senate joint hearing before the Select Committee on Intelligence and the Subcommittee on Health and Scientific Research of the Committee of Human Resources that took place on August 3, 1977, the chairman of the Health Subcommittee, Massachusetts Senator Edward M. Kennedy, stated:

> Some two years ago, the Senate Health Subcommittee heard chilling testimony about the human experimentation activities of the Central Intelligence Agency. The Deputy Director of the CIA revealed that over thirty universities and institutions were involved in an "extensive testing and experimentation" program which included covert drug tests on unwitting citizens "at all social levels, high and low, native Americans and foreign." Several of these tests involved the administration of LSD on "unwitting subjects in social situations."

The hearing revealed that there were 149 MK-ULTRA subprojects, many of which appeared to have some connection with research into "behavioural modification, drug acquisition and testing or administering drugs surreptitiously" and that the Society for the Investigation of Human Ecology (also known as the Human Ecology Foundation) was established to undertake research in the general area of the behavioural sciences. This foundation provided funding to "a lot of innocent people" who had no knowledge of the fact that this money was coming to them from the CIA. According to a March 11, 1980, report by *The Fifth Estate*, the CIA spent twenty-five years and twenty-five million dollars on secret brainwashing and mind control research under codenames like MK-ULTRA. It was through this funding that the CIA became interested in the work being done by Dr. Ewen Cameron, a professor from Albany.

Between the years of 1957 and 1961, about sixty-two thousand dollars was provided by the CIA to Dr. Cameron. But, according to a 2012 feature article in the *McGill Daily*, it all began at a clandestine meeting at the Ritz-Carleton Hotel on Sherbrooke Street on July 1, 1951, to launch a joint American-British-Canadian CIA-funded series of studies on sensory deprivation.

Dr. Donald Hebb, McGill's director of psychology, received a ten thousand dollar grant as part of this funding, in an attempt to determine the relationship between sensory deprivation and the vulnerability of a person's cognitive ability. In one study, Hebb played tapes of recorded voices expressing either pro-religious or anti-scientific sentiments to students who were isolated and deprived of most of their senses for an entire day. The students, who had previously taken stances against sentiments being expressed, came out of the experience more receptive to those same thoughts and viewpoints. The long periods of sensory deprivation appeared to make the subjects far more susceptible to perspectives that radically differed from the their previous stance.

Dr. Hebb's research helped to fuel the CIA's ongoing interest in the effects of interrogation and psychological torture. Work that, years later, Dr. Ewen Cameron would continue to conduct at McGill.

Dr. Donald Ewen Cameron

Considered an authoritative figure in psychiatric research, Dr. Donald Ewen Cameron was born in Scotland on December 24, 1901. He was

MANCHURIAN CANDIDATE

The term *Manchurian Candidate* is sometimes used when referring to such military techniques as mentioned in this chapter, and is derived from the 1959 novel *The Manchurian Candidate* by Richard Condon. Condon's novel, a political thriller, describes the fate of an American soldier (Sergeant Raymond Shaw) who is captured and brainwashed during the Korean War in 1952 in Manchuria. On his return to the United States, it is revealed that he has become an unwitting sleeper agent, puppet, and assassin for a Communist conspiracy. The novel was adapted into a film in 1962 directed by John Frankenheimer, starring Frank Sinatra, Angela Lansbury, and Janet Leigh. It was remade in 2004, directed by Jonathan Demme and starring Liev Scheiber, Denzel Washington, and Meryl Streep.

educated at Glasgow University and the University of London before working and studying in Glasgow, Switzerland, Manitoba, and Maryland. In 1936 he moved to Massachusetts to become the director of the research division at Worchester State Hospital, where he published his first book, *Objective and Experimental Psychiatry*. This book, and his research, revealed his underlying belief that psychiatry should follow a strict clinical and scientific method, with rigorous scientific principles that studied the relationship between the mind and the body, or the organic and the neurological.

Dr. Cameron was working as a professor of neurology and psychiatry in New York at Albany Medical College in 1943 when he was invited to Montreal by Dr. Wilder Penfield, Montreal's first neurosurgeon and the first director of the Montreal Neurological Institute and Hospital. As the first director of the Allan Memorial Institute and the first chairman of the Department of Psychiatry at McGill, Cameron began recruiting psychologists, biologists, and psychoanalysts from around the world, adopting an open door policy and a "day treatment" or "outpatient" concept, which were new to North America at the time.

In 1945, Dr. Cameron was invited to the Nuremberg Trials for a psychiatric evaluation of Rudolf Hess, deputy führer of the Nazi Party. It is ironic that he was involved in the judging of the atrocities of the Nazi leadership and not all that long before his own career was tainted by torments he caused others. Cameron published papers in which he decried Second World War–era Germany as an example of general anxiety and nervous tension helping to poison the minds of society. He believed that mental conditions were socially contagious and that such illnesses could be reconditioned out of a person through neurological, physiological, and biological means. This led to his experimentation with psychotic and paralytic drugs combined with electroshock therapy, in order to erase existing memories and reduce the mind to a core psyche that could then be reconstructed or reprogrammed.

Cameron was an internationally honoured and respected psychiatrist, but he wasn't liked. He was described by former colleague Dr. Elliot Emmanuel in a 1980 *Fifth Estate* interview as authoritarian, ruthless, power hungry, nervous, tense, angry, and "not very nice." Emmanuel explained that the quantity, the intensity, and the frequency with which the electroshock therapy was given by Cameron was unethical. "There was no informed consent."

Cameron suggested using chemical agents to break down ongoing patterns of behaviour, subjecting patients to terrifying LSD trips that lasted for hours. He also provided a treatment called depatterning, which involved massive rounds of electroshock. Treatments, at twenty times the intensity of those used today, were administered to patients who were kept sleeping for days. Some of the patients lost their memories, and others forgot even their earliest functions, such as basic toilet training. Depatterning also involved subjecting participants to electroshocks multiple times a day rather than two or three times over the span of a week. The goal was to reduce the patient to an animal or vegetative state. An additional experiment involved putting patients to sleep for as long as a month at a time and having repeated patterned messages play for up to fifteen hours a day while the patients were unconscious, in an attempt to brainwash the patients "back to health."

The concept behind these experimental therapeutic treatments was to completely obliterate negative memories and patterns of behaviour and infuse new positivity or an alternative to the old, undesirable behaviour. Cameron called this technique psychic driving. However, the treatments left so many patients with severe amnesia that the Allan Memorial Institute stopped the treatments after Cameron left in 1964.

Depatterning

An article written in an April 1962 issue of the journal *Comprehensive Psychiatry* titled "The Depatterning Treatment of Schizophrenia," by Dr. Cameron and two colleagues, opens with the proposition that this successful method of treatment was "imperative" because of the ongoing revolution in psychiatric hospitalization.

It goes on to state that depatterning consisted of "the administration of two to four electroshocks daily to the point where the patient developed an organic brain syndrome with acute confusion, disorientation, and interference with his learned habits of eating and bladder and bowel control." It also states that, while in this condition, the schizophrenic symptoms also disappeared.

The treatment procedure outlined the extended continuous sleep regimen, which involved the use of three barbiturates and included three temporary waking periods for meals and toilet use. Approximately three days into the sleep process a twice-daily electroshock treatment of six rapidly delivered shocks began and ran for five days, after which the six shock treatments were reduced from twice to once daily.

With respect to the treatment's efficiency, the paper states that, though it involved a significant expenditure of time and effort on behalf of the administering team, it resulted in a considerable increase in efficiency. "With regard to the detrimental side effects," the article continues, "the most serious is of course the period of complete amnesia. We are working upon methods to reduce this and it is proper to say that while it is a source of trouble and annoyance to the patient during the first six months or so following discharge, a scaffolding of subsequent memories consisting in what he had been told of events which happened during the amnestic period gradually takes form."

A CLOCKWORK ORANGE

A dystopian novel by British writer Anthony Burgess and published in 1962, *A Clockwork Orange* depicts the violent exploits of teenage Alex, his incarceration for murder, and the experimental "Ludovico Technique" that is performed on him. The experiment consists of behaviour-modification aversion-therapy treatment, which involves the injection of a nausea-inducing drug while he listens to classic music and watches graphically violent scenes. The intent of the conditioning is that he will become severely ill at the mere thought of violence. A side effect of the experiment is that hearing previously enjoyed music, such as Beethoven's *Symphony No. 9*, also results in overwhelming nausea. In an essay about the novel titled "Clockwork Oranges," Burgess explained the title as appropriate for a story about the application of Pavlovian laws to an organism which, like a fruit, was capable of sweetness and colour.

Long Term Suffering of Involuntary Patients

Patients expecting to receive the best psychiatric care that money could buy came from all over Canada to be treated by Dr. Cameron. But very few of the patients arriving were informed that the treatments being conducted on them were highly experimental. Several of Dr. Cameron's involuntary experimental subjects started to come forward in the 1980s, willing to openly discuss the various forms of bizarre and extreme therapy they received while under his care. In their testimonies, they shared the common experiences of devastating physical and mental pain, memory loss, and relentless feelings of intense anxiety and extreme isolation.

A 1992 article in the *New York Times* described a Canadian government compensation of up to eighty thousand dollars for the eighty or so Canadians who had undergone the psychic driving treatment in the '50s and '60s. In the article, Linda McDonald (one of those eighty victims), describes walking into the hospital as a healthy and coherent person with a husband on one arm and a guitar in the other. After spending almost ninety days in a sleep room and being subjected to more than one hundred shock treatments and heavy doses of barbiturates and other drugs, she emerged without the ability to play the guitar, read, or write. She suffered severe memory loss of the first twenty-six years of her life, could not remember either her husband or her five children, and had to relearn basic functions such as toilet training.

The same article quotes a retired member of Parliament, David Orlikow, discussing his then-deceased wife, Velma, who was also a victim of this barbaric treatment regimen. He said she emerged from the experiments emotionally unstable and, despite being an intelligent person, she had lost the ability to read. He also explained that there were days she would sit around doing nothing or suddenly fall into "unexplainable rages."

In a YouTube video titled "MK-ULTRA survivor speaks," Lynne Moss-Sharman, an activist and supporter of trauma victims, shared her memories of surviving the experiments as a child. She would be strapped down to a table and electricity would be applied to various parts of her body. "A simple form of torture that they used on myself and on a lot of other children was the dislocation of your limbs," Moss-Sharman says.

"So they dislocated both your arms and your legs. That was probably the simplest, easiest and cheapest way to re-enforce the notion that you were absolutely helpless and that you could do nothing physically to defend or protect yourself from what they could do to you."

An episode of *The Fifth Estate* included an interview with Bob Logie, who had been admitted to Allan Memorial at the age of eighteen for treatment of psychosomatic leg pain. Post-treatment, he described feeling as if his mind had been completely invaded, and that he might know what a guinea pig feels like. Logie said he couldn't hold down a job for very long and the anxiety continued to build. "I just felt that I couldn't cope, I couldn't adjust after the LSD," he said.

The CIA compiled research done at McGill and at other universities in the United States and Britain into the *Kubark Counterintelligence Interrogation Handbook*, which essentially could be seen as a torture manual. The text of this book is widely available via a quick internet search. One can imagine that the various torture techniques used by the U.S. military on detainees in locations like Guantanamo Bay might be derived from this text. This book is merely one way that the dark legacy of these experimental treatments conducted by Dr. Cameron continues to live on. *Transcultural Psychiatry*, a peer-reviewed academic journal that publishes papers in the fields of cultural psychiatry, psychology, and anthropology, was originally funded in the early 1960s by the CIA money. The journal, which continues to be published independently from the original funding source, is considered the official journal of the World Psychiatric Association, Transcultural Psychiatry Section, and has proven to be a much-respected source of research, insight, and knowledge. So perhaps not everything associated with the torture treatments in Montreal was painted with brushes of pure evil.

Due to new rules regarding ethics in scientific and psychological research, the type of horrid and life-altering experiments that Dr. Cameron conducted in Montreal are no longer possible. For example, in 1976 President Gerald Ford issued an Executive Order on Intelligence Activities, the first of its kind, which prohibited "experimentation with drugs on human subjects, except with the informed consent, in writing and witnessed by a disinterested party, of each such human subject."

These orders were followed by both President Carter and President Reagan with additional direction that such prohibition be applied to any form of human experimentation.

It provides some level of comfort to know that we have learned from these previous horrific experiences and that positive change has occurred to prevent it from happening again. But that doesn't change the dark legacy of what took place on the McGill campus in Montreal that still haunts both the victims and the country today.

Eight (or More) Ghosts in the Museum
Château Ramezay, Old Montreal

C hâteau Ramezay is a building full of history ... and full of ghosts. Located on Notre-Dame Street in Old Montreal, the Château has had half a dozen personas in the 313 years since it was built. Originally constructed in 1705 as a residence for Mayor Claude de Ramezay, the building has changed hands many times. It was purchased by the fur trading French East India Company in 1745. During the American Revolution it became the campaign headquarters for the Continental Army, and Benjamin Franklin stayed there overnight. It was used during the eighteenth and nineteenth centuries as a courthouse and later housed the Ministry of Public Education and the Faculty of Medicine of Laval University.

It became a museum in 1894 and remains so to this day, displaying works of art, ethnological artifacts, a coin collection, historical photographs, and antiquarian books, all chronicling the culture of Montreal through the ages. It is the oldest private history museum in the province, and in 1929 it became the first building in Quebec to be designated a historic monument.

The Château has lived many different lives since it was built, and so it follows that it now houses many different ghosts. Paranormal activity has long been reported within its walls by employees of the museum as well as visitors, each encounter similar in the unease it inspires but

Château Ramezay in the early 1900s.

singular in detail. Could each spectral event be the work of one ghost? Possibly. We'll leave it to you to decide.

Here are some of the "many" ghosts that haunt the Château Ramezay.

The Dancer

On the Paranormal Studies & Inquiry Canada website, a visitor to the Château describes hearing footsteps and a door closing as she entered the ballroom. Out of the corner of her eye she spotted a woman in period clothing leaving the room through another door. She was barely startled because there were a few costumed guides in the building. Only when she entered the ballroom fully did she realize there was no other door out of the room other than the one she'd just come through.

The Hand Washer

A museum employee arrived at work one morning, unlocked the door, and went upstairs to put his lunch in the fridge. While in the kitchen, he heard the sound of toilet paper being pulled from the roll in the women's washroom, which was odd since he thought he was alone in the building. The light in the bathroom was off, and there was no answer when he knocked. Going inside, he noticed bubbles in the sink, as though someone had just washed their hands, but there was no one in the room.

The Jacques Cartier Impersonator

There was once a young employee at the museum who was a direct descendant of Jacques Cartier. While at work one day, she heard someone calling her name from the next room. That room contains a framed portrait of Jacques Cartier. The girl was alone in the building.

The Avid Reader or the Book Hater

Upon opening the doors one morning, staff members noticed a pile of brochures scattered across the floor. On another day two books had fallen from a shelf while all the other books on the bookshelf were undisturbed. It is unlikely that an ordinary disturbance would cause just two volumes to fall from a shelf in such a way. Could they have fallen without ghostly help? If a spirit was responsible, it is difficult to know whether the spectre in question was offended by the tomes, or had read them and then left them carelessly on the floor. Either way, its interest in the written word is notable.

The Sneezer

Four technicians were preparing an exhibit after-hours when they heard a loud sneeze out in the corridor. They immediately went to see who it was, since the museum was closed. There was nobody there.

The Decorator

An employee was alone in the basement when he left a room to go check on something. When he returned just seconds later, he found six X-acto blades lying in a perfect fan shape on top of a pile of papers he'd only just put down. He was so unnerved by the experience that it was six months before he mentioned the occurrence to anyone.

The Squealers

Perhaps the strangest occurrence reported in the museum took place in 2005. Two staff members were in the basement when two chairs seemed to twist strangely, as though people of considerable weight were sitting in them. Then a strange noise began to emenate from the chairs, growing louder and higher. The noise continued for almost thirty seconds. It stopped just as suddenly as it began.

* * *

Some believe they know the identity of the Château Ramezay ghost. One museum volunteer suggests that it is the spirit of Anna O'Dowd, a live-in caretaker who died in her bathtub in 1985. The Haunted Places website names a former guard, Mr. O'Leary, as the likely candidate. It's possible the two of them together could cover all the encounters listed, if they were both heavy-set. Alternatively, there are eight ghosts — or more — haunting this historic building. Whatever the number, they may be amused that visitors who come to the museum are oblivious to the fact that the figures from history they are learning about are standing in the very same room.

Mysteries in the Montreal Skies: UFOs, Flying Saucers, and Other Unexplained Sights

In much of this book, we explore odd, eerie, and macabre things that have occurred in the shadows, on the streets, among historic landscapes, and inside buildings and homes that have stood for hundreds of years. But it's time to now pause and take a brief look at the skies above the city.

Throughout history, and among many countries and cultures, strange and unexplained objects and lights have been spotted in the sky. The term *flying saucer* was first made popular in the 1940s, and a decade later, the United States Air Force coined a phrase for the phenomenon that does not imply one particular shape. And thus the term *UFO*, or *unidentified flying object*, was born. (The French version of the term is OVNI, from the French phrase *objet volant non-identifié*.) Although the terms UFO or *flying saucer* are most commonly associated with aliens or otherworldly spacecraft, the term *unidentified flying object* is actually used to refer to an object someone observes in which the source or origin is not known.

Montreal, like so many other locales around the world, has been visited by a variety of UFOs. A number of people have spotted strange unidentified objects that they couldn't explain in the afternoon or night sky. A 2014 report by Geoff Dittman and Chris Rutkowski of the Canadian UFO Survey titled "25 Years of Canadian UFO Reports" lists the cities with the highest number of reported UFO cases. Montreal placed sixth on the list, with 287 sightings. The list ranked the cities in Canada in the following order: Toronto, Winnipeg, Vancouver, Calgary, Edmonton, Montreal. The report notes that the distribution of UFO reports isn't directly related to the population of a city; if that were the case, Montreal, being the second largest city in Canada, would be listed second.

The report's list of the top ten "strangest" UFO reports, cites the January 6, 1977, case of Ms. Florida Malboef, who reported seeing a saucer-shaped object landing on a building near her home. She said that she spotted a pair of "spindly" creatures in what looked like tight-fitting suits moving about the roof of the building before they disappeared from sight and the saucer-like object lifted off and flew away.

A 1985 *Montreal Gazette* article titled "UFO clerk blasé about sightings" shares the fact that one night authorities from Transport Canada at Dorval airport received three calls between 11:00 p.m. and 1:00 a.m. mentioning a large white- or red-looking oval object in the skies over north Montreal. The first report came from a middle-aged woman from Mount Royal, identified as Mildred, who said she was roused from her bed when the windows began to rattle as a result of what sounded like "hundreds of firecrackers" crashing over the house.

She immediately woke her husband and they went to the bedroom window and saw a fiery red ball moving slowly and low in the sky in a northeast direction. Intrigued, she threw on her kimono and went downstairs to see if she could get a better look. "From my living room I saw the big red ball; it had a beehive effect," Mildred told reporter Michael Farber. "It was very bright. It lit up the sky for an hour and a half. And there was a noise, like gunshots or firecrackers and static, static from hundreds of radios."

However, a shift manager at the air traffic control centre at Dorval said there had been post-Easter Sunday fireworks celebrations in the area, which could have explained the phenomenon. The same article included a statement by a clerk at the Hertzberg Institute, the arm of the National Research Council that studies astrophysics, who said that she was unconcerned about the incident, noting that she receives and files as many as 150 reports of UFO sightings every year, and that they were just part of the regular routine for her.

In a 1978 *Montreal Gazette* article, Marc Leduc, a physics teacher and investigator for UFO Quebec, spoke about the popularity of a movie called *Close Encounters of the Third Kind* and the increased incidents of UFO sightings since its release. He predicted that 1978 would be a peak year for UFOs over Montreal. As predicted, one of the reports was even picked up by an Ohio newspaper. A *Toledo Blade* report from 1978 titled "2 Campers Report UFO Photographs" claims that two Canadian men photographed an unidentified glowing object that hovered over a lake in La Verendrye Park while they were camping at Lake Baskatong.

They reported that the brilliant object hurtled out of the sky and seemed to disappear, but that it later returned and hovered silently over the water of the lake for about half a minute. Their photograph revealed a blurry and grainy white oval-shaped object in the middle of an expanse of black.

But Leduc, who maintained a relatively sceptical position about the twelve hundred or so reports that UFO Quebec had received between 1961 and 1978, said that some of them might actually have some substance. "I am not a believer in UFOs," he said. "But we are confronted with so much evidence that I must be open-minded." Leduc, after all, had an experience of his own that he just couldn't explain.

On August 10, 1973, Leduc was standing outside St. Bruno, which is south of Montreal, when he spotted a squadron of UFOs flashing across the sky in a northerly direction. Following up on reports from several people who had spotted objects in the sky, Leduc said that he went outside to take a look for himself. "The first thing we saw," he said, "was a green fireball, two-thirds the apparent size of the moon. Then, they were upon us — a squadron of eight UFOs, starlike in appearance, constantly passing each other and moving silently but at tremendous speed.

"They went from the south to the north of the sky in less than five seconds — as fast as a shooting star but too long-lasting to be either a shooting star or a meteor."

One of the most well-known documented UFO sightings, "the Place Bonaventure Incident," occurred on November 7, 1990. A CBC Archives report by reporter Pierre Mignault for *Newswatch* in November 1994 detailed the events of that night. At approximately 7:20 p.m., a female tourist who was swimming in the outdoor pool on the seventeenth floor of the Place Bonaventure hotel spotted what she described as a round metallic object in the sky. The unidentifiable object was emitting a series of brilliant light beams.

She called out to the pool lifeguard, who looked out and spotted the same eerie phenomenon. Not certain what to do, the lifeguard contacted the hotel's security guard, who was startled by the inexplicable sight and contacted both the police and a reporter from the *La Presse* newspaper. The reporter, Gilles Beliveau, and a police officer arrived at the same time and rode up in the same elevator to the pool, the two of them joking about the alleged incident, assuming it would turn out to be a humorous misunderstanding.

"When we arrived together on the roof," Beliveau said, "he looked in the sky and said 'Sacrement.' He was astonished, like I was." ("Sacrament" is a common French-Canadian curse that translates roughly to "goddamn.")

The officer said, "We saw this round shape, it seemed metallic. It projected light beams. It had four series of three light beams each. It was gigantic."

The head of the police, who was called in, arrived at about 9:00 p.m. and reached out to the local military and airports to determine if there were operations being performed in nearby airspace. They all confirmed that nothing of the sort was taking place. The RCMP and NASA were also contacted about the unexplainable sighting, which lasted for almost three full hours.

Another eyewitness, who was driving just a few miles away, said he also saw a large light-emitting object at about the same time. He described pulling off the road to get a better look and hearing a low-frequency purring-like sound as if from an engine. He described the object as remaining "very static" before suddenly gliding to another position.

A meteorologist who looked into the phenomenon concluded that the eyewitnesses must have been seeing the Northern Lights. However, a detailed report disputes this allegation. The event caught the attention of Bernard Guénette, a Montreal-based UFO researcher, who, together with Dr. Richard Haines, a former scientist from NASA, published a twenty-five-page report in 1992 about the incident. Their report concluded that evidence of the existence of an approximately 540-metre-wide, highly unusual, hovering, silent object was indisputable. "There is nothing about these particular meteorological conditions," the report continued, "that could produce an optical effect of the kind described by these witnesses."

The 2016 Canadian UFO survey indicates that 1,131 UFO reports were officially filed in Canada that year, above a thousand cases for the fifth year in a row. The report continues that Montreal, with seventy-three reports, was the city with the most number of UFO reports for that year. It indicates that of all the reports across Canada, 74 percent of them had insufficient evidence, 1 percent of them were explainable, 4 percent of them were unexplained, and 21 percent of them were defined as "probable."

This suggests that as many as one in every four UFO sighting reported are truly unexplained phenomenon. Whether the objects, lights, and sightings in the sky are evidence of extraterrestrial life-forms visiting earth, or they are an indication of some other yet-to-be-explained phenomenon, at least eighteen of the seventy-three reports from Montreal from 2016 appear to have enough substance to make even a skeptic look up to the skies and wonder.

Maud: The Willow Inn Ghost
Hudson, Quebec

Residents of Hudson, an off-island suburb to the west of Montreal, have all heard of Maud. She's the ghost who haunts the iconic Willow Inn, a striking building first constructed in 1820 as a private home and later used as a general store before becoming a pub and inn. But who is Maud? Does she actually haunt the Willow Inn, as she's been said to for so long, or is she just an urban legend conjured up to keep the tourists interested? Did Maud ever really exist at all?

The story begins in 1837. In *Ghost Stories of Canada*, John Robert Colombo reports that the inn was used as a meeting place for the Patriotes as they planned the Battle of Saint-Eustache, an important battle in the Lower Canada Rebellion (1837–1838) that would see the British defeat the rebels of Quebec. Maud, a servant girl loyal to the British, was caught eavesdropping on one of their meetings. As it was believed she couldn't be trusted, the rebels murdered her and buried her body in the basement. But that was not the end of Maud.

For many years, guests of the Willow Inn have experienced strange phenomenon. According to the Hudson Historical Society, stacks of rocks are routinely discovered outside of Room 8, where the meeting of the Patriotes took place. Maud is heard singing in the hallways. Objects fall over, seemingly by themselves, and the basement door slams shut of its own accord — apparently as Maud returns to her body's resting

Condemned by the British as rebels, celebrated by the French-Canadian population as heroes, the men hanged in 1839 for their activities in the 1837 Rebellion remain celebrated figures. In Pendaison de cinq Patriotes au Pied-du-Courant, *they are commemorated by the French-Canadian artist Henri Julien.*

place. Some people have even said they've smelled Maud's perfume. The yearly haunting tends to take place between Halloween and the end of November, right around the time Maud was allegedly killed.

Eerie stuff indeed, and certainly a compelling story, but is there any truth to it? A local historian named Rob Hodgson thinks not. In a 2017 Global News article, Hodgson claims there never was a servant girl named Maud, and that in fact the whole story was made up by the owners in the 1970s to attract some attention to their inn. The only Maud who ever lived or died at the Willow Inn was one Maud Leger, the mother of the owner who passed in 1960, more than a hundred years after the Patriotes lost the Battle of Saint-Eustache.

It should also be pointed out that the original Willow Inn burned down in a fire in 1989 and was rebuilt later that year in the exact same style, only larger. It went through extensive renovations from 2016 to 2017 under new ownership. Would a ghost continue to haunt a building just because it

The Willow Inn, as it looks today. The original structure burned down in 1989 and was rebuilt in the same style.

resembles the one she died in and sits on the same land? Or is it her grave she is tethered to, which possibly remained untouched by the flames?

In an effort to put the questions surrounding the veracity of the Maud story to rest, a team of paranormal researchers led by Dan Ducheneaux did their own investigation of the Willow Inn in the summer of 2017. After spending two nights in the inn with all their gear, Ducheneaux and his team couldn't definitively rule out a paranormal presence in the building. They reported to Global News that they had heard a child's voice calling out "one." There were no children staying at the inn at the time and the owner claimed it's unlikely they could have heard voices from the street. Rather more alarming was the sound they heard of an old woman either laughing or crying at the very moment their heat sensors went off.

Ducheneaux was uneasy about being on the second floor for most of the night. He believes *something* is going on at the inn, be it the restless ghost of Maud roaming the halls, or another explanation.

Though hardly a ringing endorsement, this modern investigation will surely keep the story of Maud, the ghost of Willow Inn, alive. Real or imaginary, her ghostly presence will live on in Hudson and beyond for years to come.

Careful, This One Bites: Wayne Clifford Boden, "The Vampire Rapist"

He didn't look like a vampire. Wayne Clifford Boden was a charming twenty-three-year-old Montrealer with a boyish look and winning smile when he went on a killing spree beginning in the late 1960s. It ended with five young women raped, murdered, and bitten. That's right, Boden, also known as the Vampire Rapist, had the bizarre modus operandi of biting his victims on their breasts, leaving behind dental evidence which eventually led to his arrest and conviction.

You might be tempted to dismiss Boden as a pop-culture fanatic, spurred on by the trend toward vampires on TV and the silver screen, and convinced by some inner madness to allow his bloody impulses free in real life. Remember, however, this was decades ago, long before *Twilight*, or *The Vampire Diaries*, or *Interview with the Vampire*. So, what was it that pushed Boden to not only murder, but deliver the dark kiss? Could it be that he was in fact a real-life vampire?

There is some debate as to which victim was Boden's first. In *The Serial Killer Files*, Harold Schechter asserts that schoolteacher Norma Vaillancourt was the first to go, in July 1968. The twenty-one-year-old was raped and strangled to death in her apartment, with bite marks covering her breasts. The police found no sign of a struggle, either on the deceased's body or in the apartment, implying that Vaillancourt had let her killer in. Oddly, the dead girl was found with a smile on her face.

Next to go, nearly a year later, was Shirley Audette, whose body was dumped behind an apartment complex downtown. Though she had been raped, strangled, and bitten on the breasts — exactly like Norma Vaillancourt — her body was fully clothed when found and there were no signs of a struggle.

In November of 1969, it happened again. Marielle Archambault, a young employee at a downtown jewellery shop, was found by her employer after she didn't show up for work. She was in her apartment, dead, raped, and bitten. This time, however, it seemed some kind of struggle had occurred, as the apartment was a mess and Archambault's clothes were ripped. Though such a fight might make one think Archambault had been attacked by a stranger, Schechter claims the police were led to believe otherwise when they found a crumpled photo of a good-looking young man at the scene. Archambault's co-workers identified the man as Bill, a guy they'd seen the dead girl chatting with that very day.

Jean Way was almost saved. Her boyfriend came to pick her up for a date on the day she died. When she didn't answer the door he left and returned an hour later, by which time the poor girl was dead. It's believed Boden was in the apartment with Way when the boyfriend first came by and, alarmed by his knock on the door, fled the scene. This would explain the fact that Way's body was left naked and her breasts were unmolested, unlike the other victims. She had been raped and strangled, though. Boden left before he could finish the job. One thing to note about Jean Way is that skin was found under her fingernails. She might not have won, but she fought back.

Perhaps intuiting that he wasn't going to get away with it much longer in Montreal, Boden trekked across the country to Calgary to carry out his final murder on May 18, 1971. Elizabeth Porteous, a thirty-three-year-old teacher, met her end like the rest. One final clue was left behind: A cufflink hidden underneath her body. Schechter reports that Porteous's friends knew she was dating a man named Bill, and that he drove a blue Mercedes. It was this car, in the end, that led to Boden's apprehension, when the police spotted it near Porteous's apartment and nabbed the killer as he was walking toward it the very next day.

Boden, now in police custody, didn't confess right away. He admitted to going by the name Bill and taking Porteous on a date on the night of her murder, but insisted she had been perfectly fine when he'd left her. Yes, the cufflink was his, but he was no killer. But as he resembled the man in the photo found in Archambault's apartment, the police held him anyway on suspicion of murder.

It was the bite marks that did him in. At his trial for the murder of Elizabeth Porteous, a local orthodontist was able to prove through bite mark evidence that the marks on Porteous's body could not have been made by anyone but Boden. Boden's conviction was the first in North America to be made by forensic odontological evidence, the same method that would eventually take down Ted Bundy.

For Porteous's murder, Boden was sentenced to life in prison.

Boden eventually confessed to the Montreal murders, as well, save that of Vaillancourt, which he claimed to know nothing about, though hers was the death that started it all. For the rapes and killings of Audette, Archambault, and Way, Boden was given an additional three life sentences.

No explanation was ever given by Wayne Boden as to why he bit his victim's breasts, nor did he ever claim to be a vampire — an interesting defence and one that would surely have turned his court case into a circus — but one cannot deny that he did seem to have some of the characteristics commonly attributed to them. Aren't vampires known to be young, good-looking, and able to use their charms to get the girl into their arms before baring their fangs? It would explain how he managed to get into his victim's apartments — a vampire can't force his way in. He has to be invited.

Wild imagining aside, Boden, who died in prison in 2006, was an evil man, a serial killer with a strange quirk, and a murderer who eventually got what he deserved.

The One-Legged Ghost of Jack McLean
Mount Royal

The McGill students living in Molson Hall have all heard the rumours. Don't go into the woods alone at night, they whisper. Ignore those strange sounds you hear coming out of the dark. Sometimes senior students trick first-year students into believing there's a cable car that goes up the mountain. "Haven't you seen it going by?" they ask, their eyes shining with mischief. "Don't you hear the clicking of the cars at night?"

The woods surrounding the Olmsted trail on Mount Royal are haunted, and the story of how a ghost came to live there begins decades ago, with the opening of the Mount Royal Funicular Railway. Opened in 1895, the funicular was a popular attraction that ran for almost twenty-five years in Mount Royal Park. It consisted of cable cars on rails that ran up and down the mountain at a forty-degree angle. Starting near the current McConnell Arena and running all the way to the peak, the funicular allowed riders to enjoy spectacular views of the city. The cost of a ride was five cents to go up, and twenty-five people could ride at a time. Excited visitors boarded the cars in droves when the attraction first opened. Little did they know that just steps from where they stood there would soon be a gruesome discovery.

As described on the Haunted Mountain walk conducted by Haunted Montreal, it was July 1896 when a park guard came upon a dead body covered by a curtain near the start of the rail line. When he pulled the curtain away he noticed that the man had had one of his legs amputated, but this detail was entirely forgotten when he was confronted by another far more horrifying sight: The dead man's face was horribly burned, his jaw agape, his features nearly unrecognizable. His lips were blistered, his skin destroyed, and, worst of all, his trachea was burned clear through. An awful odour that reminded the guard of tar was emanating from the corpse's face.

When the body was thoroughly examined, it was discovered that a handkerchief drenched in carbolic acid had been stuffed down the man's throat and the death was ruled a suicide. Those wanting to take their own lives often used carbolic acid, a common household disinfectant at the turn of the century. Death by carbolic acid is agonizing but swift, producing a quick succession of intense pain, vomiting, paralysis, and coma until the heart stops beating. So, who was this poor soul who'd chosen such a grisly end?

The identification in his pocket listed him as John "Jack" McLean, a once-famous athlete who had played for the McGill football team. Married with two children, Jack had taken on a second job as a train changer to make some extra money. One day while doing his job on the train tracks, Jack's foot became stuck in the rails as a train was going by, severing his leg. The injury summarily ended his athletic career and sank Jack into a terrible depression. He was often seen hobbling around the park on his crutches and getting drunk among the trees. Some even reported seeing him climbing the cable car rails while the funicular was in operation, though how he could have done so with his injury remains to be seen. Then one day Jack decided he could no longer stand to live and took a bottle of carbolic acid to the park.

After Jack's death, strange things began to happen to the funicular. The cars began to break down for no apparent reason. Sometimes the metal cables that pulled the cars up and down would snap, again without any apparent cause, and the fire brigade would have to be called to rescue stranded, terrified passengers. White orbs of light could be seen floating in the woods around the tracks at night.

The funicular was taken out of commission in 1918 and its metal rails sold to a recycling company (there was a shortage of metal after

The Mount Royal Funicular, circa 1900. To the left of the tracks is where the McGill residence halls now stand.

the First World War). But the end of the funicular was not the end of the funicular's ghost.

There are several McGill residences next to the path where the funicular once ran, and the students who live there consistently report strange occurrences. Orbs are often seen floating in the canopy of the forest. A male voice can be heard crying for help in the night. When it's late and everyone is sleeping, the sound of grinding and clicking metal can be heard, as though a cable car is passing by.

In 2012, a student was walking on the path in the evening after class. A man wearing a heavy cloak approached her out of the dark and took her firmly by the shoulders. Startled and feeling the first tendrils of fear, the student pulled out her cellphone for some light, as the path was only dimly lit. Brandishing her phone, she turned it on to reveal the man's face and gasped at what she saw, for his skin was puckered and burned and there were holes right through his neck. He seemed to be struggling to speak, and as he opened his mouth pleadingly, she turned on her heel and ran.

Murdered by the Mob: Organized Crime in Montreal

L ike any large North American city with a long history, Montreal has its share of gangsters, gamblers, mobsters, and mafiosi fighting for control of the city's illegal activities. As a major port, Montreal has been more popular than most, and it has been a fought-over locale for organized crime syndicates over the years. Of course, when the mob moves in, murder inevitably follows. To describe every ghastly homicide committed by mafia members over the years would be an impossible and stomach-turning task. But here, in no particular order, are just a few noteworthy murders carried out by the mob.

Harry Davis, Jewish Mob Boss, 1946

During the '30s and '40s, when gambling was illegal in Canada, the underground gambling operations in Montreal were mainly run by the Jewish mafia. In 1946 Harry Davis was the "edge man," the boss of the Jewish mafia. He was also involved in drug smuggling, for which he had served twelve years in prison at Montreal's St-Vincent-de-Paul Penitentiary. His former partner, Charles "Charlie" Feigenbaum, testified against him, and it's believed that Davis ordered Feigenbaum's murder. That hit was one of the first gambling-related homicides to occur in the city, but it was certainly not the last.

When Davis was released from prison in 1945, there was no new boss in power, and he quickly moved in to fill the empty spot. Reopening his gambling parlour at 1224 Stanley Street, Davis took control of all gambling in Montreal, forcing anyone who wanted to get in on the game to go through him first.

One such person was Louis Berkowitz, who wanted to open an illegal bookmaking business. Believing there were already too many of them in operation, Davis denied his request and burned down his place on Mansfield Street for good measure. Things escalated quickly after that. After hearing that Berkowitz was coming after him, Davis put out a hit on him. But not soon enough. On July 25, 1946, Berkowitz met up with Davis and shot him to death in his gambling parlour. Shortly thereafter he confessed to the murder to the editor of the *Montreal Herald*, Ted McCormick, hoping this would somehow get him a shorter sentence. He would eventually serve twelve years.

After Davis's death, the Montreal underworld was in chaos. The public was outraged to learn that organized crime had such a tight hold on their city, and the police began to crack down in earnest. This led to a brief slowdown in the city's illegal operations, though hardly an end.

James MacDonald, West End Gang Hitman, 1969

You wouldn't be able to guess that Andrew's Pub on Guy Street was once the site of a vicious gangster killing, but it was. It was 1969 and the place had a different name — The Cat's Den Lounge — and it just happened to be the headquarters of the West End Gang, Montreal's Irish mafia.

On March 15, just two days before St. Patrick's Day, the place was packed when two men came in from the fire escape. One held a revolver, and the other an M-1 machine gun. They wasted no time approaching James MacDonald, a large man known to be an enforcer for the West End Gang. Perhaps the trio exchanged words, or perhaps they didn't. All we know for sure is that moments later the M-1 was unleashed and MacDonald was hit seventeen times, his torso ripped to pieces and his brains spewed across the bar.

The killers (some believe they were themselves members of the West End Gang who suspected MacDonald was about to turn informant) then fled the scene, tossing the machine gun in the parking lot. In the end, no arrests were ever made, because no one in the bar would admit to having seen a thing.

If you visit Andrew's Pub today, it's unlikely you'll witness a mafia gun battle, but you might just get a whiff of blood and gunpowder in the air. It's said that every few years a patron reports smelling these scents. Some say they feel as though they've been bumped into from behind by a large person, but when they turn around there's no one there. Others have claimed that glancing in one of the bar's mirrors, they've seen a man stumbling around behind them, headless and reaching out to grab them. But again, when they turned around, there was no such person to be seen. This can't be James MacDonald, lingering at the bar for just the right moment to enact his final revenge. Or can it?

The Brossard Massacre: The Dubois Brothers, 1975

In 1975, the worst crime ever seen on the South Shore of Montreal was committed by the Dubois brothers. This gang, led by nine brothers of the French-Canadian Dubois family, was known for its involvement in prostitution, drugs, and loansharking. It was once referred to as the most influential criminal group on the island, and at its height was feared by both the motorcycle gangs and the mafia.

The conflict that would lead to the murders in Brossard began when the McSweens gang, who had previously worked with the Dubois brothers, tried to branch out on their own. In the violence that followed gang boss Jacques McSween was shot and killed, and two members of the Dubois gang were murdered in retaliation. The Dubois brothers were out for blood, and it all came to a head on February 13, the night before Valentine's Day.

Three masked Dubois gang members entered the bar in Hotel Lapiniere just a few minutes before midnight. It was country music night, and there were about fifty people inside. Interestingly, they came in just as there was a pause in the music, and a mime had taken the stage to entertain the crowd. As a part of his act, the mime was shooting off a fake gun when the real shooting started, causing some in the crowd to believe the noise was just a part of the act. But the bullets the gangsters sprayed into the crowd were very real.

In the end, four men were killed, including the doorman, a cab driver, and a waiter. Roger Letourneau, one of the targets and the then leader of the McSweens, was shot twelve times and killed. The shooters got away but later Pierre McSween would claim that Roger Fontaine had been among them. Fontaine was found dead in his camper a year later. He had been shot in the head and the camper set on fire.

The Lennoxville Massacre: The Hells Angels, 1985

In the early '80s the Montreal Hells Angels was divided into two chapters: the Montreal North chapter based in Laval, and the Montreal South chapter, which was oddly not based in Montreal, but in Sorel, Quebec. The Laval chapter was known for being wild and unruly, often using the drugs they were supposed to sell, and behaving like typical bikers. The Sorel chapter, by contrast, was better disciplined and more inclined to act like elite drug dealers and businessmen. They decided that something had to be done about the Laval chapter, before their aggression and run-ins with the law did real damage to the Hells Angels in Quebec.

In a secret meeting held in Sorel in 1985, the leaders of the Halifax, Sherbrooke, and South Montreal chapters came to the decision that the Montreal North chapter needed to be purged. A party was planned for March 23 at the Sherbrooke chapter's Lennoxville clubhouse as a ruse to get the North chapter all in one place for the brutal bloodbath.

Five Montreal North chapter members, including its leader, were ambushed that day. They were surrounded by forty-one men and shot to death in the clubhouse. Two other members were forced to retire, and two more were told join the Sorel chapter or die. The Laval clubhouse was looted and the five bodies were wrapped in sleeping bags, weighted down with metal plates, and dumped into the St. Lawrence River.

The Lennoxville Massacre was considered extreme and vicious, even by criminal standards, as these Hells Angels members had slaughtered their own. Dissatisfaction with these actions led to the creation of the rival biker gang the Rock Machine in 1986. The Quebec Hells Angels and the Rock Machine would later take part in the Quebec Biker War, a violent turf war that would last eight years.

The Italian Mafia Murders

Since the 1950s, the Sicilian mafia has been the dominant criminal organization in the city, with their leaders ruling Montreal's underworld. One of the most notorious of these was Nicolo Rizzuto. To describe even a small portion of the hits the Rizzuto clan has been involved in during the past sixty-odd years would be impossible, but here are the bullet point (pun intended) murder "highlights," presented to you in chronological order.

Pietro Sciarra, Paolo Violi's consigliere: Shot dead as he left the Riviera theatre where he'd seen *The Godfather* (1976). Sciarra was a snitch who betrayed the Rizzuto family. His death was the first in a series of murders to hit the Violi clan.

Francesco Violi, a brother of Paolo Violi: Gunned down in the office of Violi Importing and Distributing while his brother was in jail (1977). Francesco had taken over leadership of the Violis while his brother was in prison.

Paolo Violi, the head of the Cotroni faction of the Montreal mob: Shot in the head while playing cards at a café two months after getting out of jail (1978). Violi's killers, all Rizzuto associates, were given short sentences for the killing. Paolo Violi's death ended the reign of the Violis in Montreal, and allowed that of the Rizzutos to begin.

Rocco Violi, another brother of Paolo Violi: Shot in his kitchen by a sniper (1980). Rocco was the last of the Violi brothers. His death has often been deemed unnecessary, as he was not an important figure in the Violi clan.

Nicolo Rizzuto Jr., a grandson of the Rizzuto patriarch: Gunned down on a residential street in the Notre-Dame-de-Grâce neighbourhood in broad daylight at the age of forty (2009). He was allegedly killed by Haitian street gang leader Ducarme (Kenny) Joseph, who himself was shot and killed in 2014. Rizzuto Jr.'s death was seen as a definite challenge to Rizzuto rule, and sparked a mob war that went on for five years.

Agostino Cuntrera, acting boss of the Rizzuto clan while Vito Rizzuto was in prison: Shot outside a whole food warehouse in Saint-Léonard, aged sixty-six (2010). Cuntrera was one of the gangsters implicated in Paolo Violi's murder years before.

Nicolo Rizzuto, patriarch of the Rizzuto crime family: Killed in his Cartierville mansion by a sniper at the age of eighty-six (2010). Rizzuto's killing was the most high-profile of the mob war. His alleged killer, hitman Salvatore "Sam" Calautti, was killed in 2013.

Salvatore Montagna, the boss of the New York Bonanno crime family, which was attempting to take over the Montreal Mafia: Shot and then drowned in the Assomption River (2011). Montagna was believed to have been involved in the recent Rizzuto killings. A Rizzuto associate was charged with his murder.

Lorenzo Giordano, a high-ranking member of the Rizzuto clan: Shot in his parked car in Laval, three months after being released from prison (2016).

Rocco Sollecito, a high-ranking member of the Rizzuto clan: Shot driving his BMW SUV in broad daylight (2016). Sollecito and Giordano were two of six men vying for leadership of the disordered Montreal mafia.

* * *

Organized crime is alive and well in Montreal. Though a 2009 police crackdown on drug trafficking, which resulted in over 150 arrests, had the Hells Angels laying low for a time, a number of recent raids on member homes and clubhouses have proven that their illegal activities continue. The Rizzutos may not be as strong as they once were, but two of their leaders, Leonardo Rizzuto and Stefano Sollecito, were recently brought up on charges of gangsterism (they were eventually acquitted and released). The West End Gang lives on. Average Montrealers may remain largely oblivious, but organized crime continues to operate all around them, and hits are still being carried out all the time. So, keep your eyes and ears open, citizens. You never know who might be next on the mob's never-ending hit list.

Give Ghosts a Chance
The Queen Elizabeth Hotel

In 1969 John Lennon and Yoko Ono staged their legendary "bed-in" in room 1742 of the Queen Elizabeth Hotel in Montreal. This two-week stint in the hotel was part of an ongoing "sit-in" style protest of America's involvement in the Vietnam War. This event led to the release of Lennon's first solo single, "Give Peace a Chance," a song that has become an ongoing anthem for anti-war movements and protesters.

The hotel also has another claim to fame: a mysterious guest who seems to have never checked out. There are multiple reports of an eerie "Lady in White" who has been seen wandering the hallways and occasionally making an appearance inside rooms in the hotel.

The downtown hotel, which was built by the Canadian National Railway and opened in 1958, boasts one thousand and thirty-nine rooms on its twenty-one floors. It is the largest hotel in Quebec and, behind the Royal York in Toronto, is the second-largest Fairmont hotel in Canada.

A Paranormal Studies and Inquiry Canada article reports that one particular hotel guest claimed that they had experienced spirit phenomenon in their room. They explained that they didn't feel threatened by the presence, but that, starting at about 6:00 a.m. they heard what sounded like a person pacing back and forth beside the bed and around the room, as well as the sounds of movement inside the bathroom.

This unidentified hotel guest said that they heard something that almost sounded like a person involved in the ritual of getting up and getting ready for their day. Then, they explained, there was a sudden physical push as if someone had struck the mattress. They said that the message to them was quite clear: It was time to get up and get the hell out of bed.

There are several ideas about the identity of this spectral guest. In their book *Haunted America*, Michael Norman and Beth Scott detail the story of Pierrete Champoux, a distinguished writer and broadcaster, who had been attending a gathering of journalists at a convention at the Queen Elizabeth Hotel on Saturday, November 18, 1961. During her stay, something truly uncanny happened.

When she was on her way outside to take a short break from the events, the touch of a hand on her arm caught her attention. She turned to see writer Émile-Charles Hamel, a good friend she had not seen for quite some time. Hamel reached out and kissed her hand and the two spoke at length about the various experiences and work they had each been engaged in. According to Champoux, Hamel told her that he had "a great deal of work" he had to do at the time. She felt that there was certainly something on his mind, since he appeared a bit distracted during their conversation. After a few more pleasantries, they shook hands and parted ways.

She thought nothing of the incident until, a couple of days later, Champoux's sister mentioned that she had read in the newspaper that their mutual friend Émile-Charles Hamel had unexpectedly passed away that Saturday morning, hours before Champoux had spoken to him. She told her sister that the newspaper must have made a mistake. She had, after all, had a lengthy conversation with the man that very morning at the Queen Elizabeth Hotel.

"It isn't as if I merely recognized him across the dining room," Champoux exclaimed. "He stopped me as I was leaving, he kissed my hand and we chatted together for quite a time."

Champoux confirmed the time of death with the hospital. The only explanation for what had happened, she felt, was that Hamel had, beyond his mortal time on this earth, stopped in at a gathering of other writers and had engaged in this one final parting with a dear old friend.

Other unexplained phenomena have been reported at the hotel over the years, including mysterious knocks and echoing footsteps, disembodied voices, cold spots, and people being pushed, shoved, or touched by unseen hands. Could the Queen Elizabeth Hotel be haunted by more than memories of the infamous bed-in by Lennon and Ono? Thousands of hotels around the world are purported to be haunted by some sort of resident spirit or spirits. Hotel rooms, having seen a multitude of guests and an entire range of various emotional states — loneliness, anger, love, hate, passion, angst — are among the most probable locations to capture at least some essence of residual energy over the years.

The hotel was closed for more than a year between the summer of 2016 and 2017 for extensive renovations, but the true believer knows that no remodelling, no upgrades, and no reimagining of the decor (unless an exorcist was involved), can shake the ghosts and residual energy that might still be lingering in the hallways and suites, like the ear-worm lyrics of a beloved song.

The Missing Village of Hochelaga
The Dawson Site, Downtown Montreal

In 1534 Jacques Cartier sailed to the new world under a commission from the king of France to find a western passage to Asia. He planted a cross on the shores of Gaspé, claiming for France the land that would become Canada, and returned home believing he had discovered an Asian island. But we are most interested in his second trip in 1535, when he returned to Canada and sailed up the St. Lawrence River to land finally at the village of Hochelaga.

In a *Montreal Gazette* article, Marian Scott describes the joyous welcome Cartier and his men received from the Inidgenous inhabitants of Hochelaga. The people danced around the visitors and showered them with cornbread and fish. So much food was thrown into the longboats that it seemed to be raining bread, Cartier wrote in his records. He also gives an account of the village, which he described as being surrounded by a circular palisade that was ten metres high. Inside, there were at least fifty bark-covered longhouses that sheltered about 1,500 people. It was situated among cornfields at the foot of a mountain Cartier named Mount Royal.

Cartier's descriptions of the village are vivid and there is no reason to doubt their veracity. There is a bit of a mystery about his description, however — it is the only existing written account of Hochelaga. The reason for this is simple: no other European ever saw the village. When Samuel de Champlain returned to the area in 1603, all traces of the village had vanished.

Mount Royal Park. Jacques Cartier arriving at Hochelaga in 1535.

Ever since Champlain's visit, questions have lingered about the missing village of Hochelaga. What happened to its people? Where exactly was it located? Did it ever exist at all?

If we skip ahead 250 years, we have our first clue. In 1860 remains were discovered by constructions workers digging below Sherbrooke Street, between Metcalfe and Mansfield. Marian Scott reports that a large number of skeletons were found, as well as tools, pots, and fire-pits. Principal of McGill and pioneer geologist John William Dawson was brought in to explore and evaluate the site, and he came to the conclusion that the former village of Hochelaga had finally been found. The area was thereafter called the Dawson site.

But doubts remained. The Dawson site was much smaller than the grand village Cartier spoke of. Could the village that was unearthed be a different one entirely?

A hundred years later anthropologists Bruce Trigger and James Pendergast set out to examine this very question. Using the carbon dating available in 1972, they were able to determine that the remains did hail from the 1500s. They were unable, however, to definitively confirm that this village was Hochelaga.

Who the Indigenous people living in Hochelaga were and where they went are other unanswered questions. They were long believed to be Haudenosaunee, but Trigger and Pendergast identified them instead as St. Lawrence Iroquoians, a separate nation entirely. In their book *Family Life in Native America*, James and Dorothy Volo explain that neither the Wyandot nor the Kanien'keha:ka, both of whom believe the St. Lawrence Iroquoians to be part of their ancestry, have a story explaining the disappearance of the people of Hochelaga. Trigger and Pendergast were, however, able to find an elderly man who recounted a story told to him by his father, in which the Wyandot drove his ancestors from the country. According to this story, the nation split, some going southeast to the Abenaki, others southwest to the Haudenosaunee, and still others straight west to other Wyandot.

But does this explain the complete disappearance of the village they were leaving behind?

The search for the missing village of Hochelaga continues to this day. An archeological effort between McGill and Université de Montréal began in the summer of 2017 and was aimed at finally finding the village, with digs planned for Outremont Park, the grounds of McGill, Jeanne-Mance Park, Beaver Lake, and other locations. Construction on de Maisonneuve Boulevard West, at the southern edge of the Dawson site, was recently halted due to concerns about the destruction of artifacts. Interest in the missing village clearly remains.

We may never know much more about the villagers Cartier and his men encountered over 480 years ago. Were they simply nomadic and eventually moved on? Did Cartier miscalculate his location? If so, was the nation he encountered never located in Montreal at all? Or was it a ghost village even when Cartier landed there, already long destroyed, inhabited by spectres so convincingly real that Cartier could not tell the difference? Did the explorer feast with the dead on that fateful voyage in 1535? We may never truly know.

Not Too-Tall Tales of a Radio Station Ghost
Former CHOM-FM Building, Westmount

R adio is synonymous with disembodied voices, those almost-spectral companions whose words accompany us when we wake up, perhaps on our commute in to work, throughout our work and leisure days, or our car rides. Along with us no matter where we roam or what we are doing, they are welcomed into our lives; a part of our rituals, there like the most reliable of friends.

Sometimes, though, there are other voices on the radio. So what happens when the disc jockeys and radio station personalities encounter an equally pervasive presence, something seen, heard, and felt in eerie glimpses, odd sounds, and chillingly unexplainable cold spots?

Rather than "turning up the volume," as a DJ might do upon putting on a new hit, they might, instead, call in an exorcist.

Which is exactly what happened in 1978 at CHOM-FM in Montreal.

CHOM-FM's station slogan is "The spirit of rock." For a while, one might have forgiven the DJs if they replaced that with the phrase "the spirit of the departed" instead. We are referring to the deceased, rather than the retired, such as Robert Wagenaar, who in the fall of 2017 decided to hang up his headphones after forty illustrious years on the airwaves, most of them at CHOM-FM. An unforgettable presence (whose moniker, "Tootall," was based on the man's tall stature), he became synonymous with classic and progressive rock music in the city for more than one generation of Montrealers.

In his decades of working at the station, Tootall regularly encountered such rock legends as Kate Bush, David Bowie, Frank Zappa, Supertramp, and Genesis. But he also, on a fittingly dark and eerie night in the 1970s, bumped into a ghost who had been seen roaming the building.

In a 2014 *Montreal Gazette* article, writer Mark Abley reported a conversation that he had with the legendary broadcaster, who described a time when the station moved from 1310 Greene Avenue to a beautiful old three-storey greystone across the street at 1355 Greene.

That was when the eerie encounters with a ghost began, described by many eyewitnesses as a man wearing a green top, in various locations on and near the third floor. The apparition was sometimes seen walking up the stairway in the middle of the night, when the station was relatively deserted. Others claimed they saw the haunted eyes of the man staring back at them from a mirror in the bathroom on the third floor. DJs were left confused over how their turntable's arm was, for no discernable reason, "skipping merrily" back and forth over an album all on its own.

In the *Gazette* article, Tootall recounted a meeting with a radio announcer who had just finished his stint on the overnight program. "He was seriously pale and shaken by the strange events that had happened on his shift," Tootall said. "I believe water taps were being turned on and off, and [my] coffee cup kept mysteriously emptying."

Quite often, the ghost was associated with a feeling of intense cold, centralized near the music library on the building's third floor. A look into the building's history might explain a bit about this reported phenomenon that was so well-known that the radio station was featured in an August 1984 article in the *National Enquirer* entitled "Radio Station Spooked by Tormented Ghost."

The beautiful old building that was serving as the station's new location came with a tale of tragedy, according to Rob Braide, program director at CHOM-FM, who was a guest on the "Ghostly Radio Tales" episode of the *Radio Stuff Podcast*, hosted by Larry Gifford, in October 2017. In that episode, Braide shared some of the tales he had heard over the years, as well as a tragic story about a suicide. A homeowner, a man who was apparently distraught and going through an unpleasant and messy divorce, descended into alcoholism and eventually took his own life with a shotgun in the back bedroom on the top floor of the building — a space that eventually became the music library next to the studio.

The man was apparently wearing a green sweater the day he died, which may explain why the colour green was a common element of the spectral image sometimes seen sitting in the announcer's chair at the console in the station. Braide said that morning show host Daniel Richler (son of Mordecai Richler) "was completely freaked out by the whole thing and ... ended up ... leaving [partially] because of it."

Braide also said that some people claimed that they had seen a head on the top of the vending machine and two feet sticking out of the bottom. But he suggested that this particular vision might have more to do with the smoke of a green plant regularly associated with a rock musician's lifestyle.

Despite the tragic and violent end of life of the building's previous owner, the ghost itself wasn't seen by radio station staff as evil. "It was never considered a malevolent figure," Braide explained. "He was just kind of there." But that presence was enough to prompt radio station personnel to seek the services of an exorcist.

Tootall explained that in 1978 the office manager hired a psychic and pictures of Jesus were hung in various locations in the building to see if those actions would help to chase the spirit away. That same year an exorcism was staged in an attempt to finally rid the building of the CHOM-FM ghost. "That was something else," Tootall told reporter Bill Brownstein of the *Montreal Gazette*.

Of course, not all of the stories associated with the ghost were eerie and unexplained. One of the most memorable frights, Braide explained, were just the result of bad timing, or perhaps perfect timing, depending on your perspective. One night, a pair of priests, a woman considered the "den mother" of the station, and the owner's son were in the music library performing an exorcism at midnight. Braide and other employees knew to stay away from that area so the group could complete their task. But later on, in the wee morning hours, Braide needed to enter the library to retrieve a Pink Floyd record. He figured that they would have completed their ritual and left hours earlier; but when he burst through the door, they all screamed and jumped out of their seats. It turned out they were in the middle of using a Ouija board to try to communicate with the dead man's spirit.

Everyone who came through the station always mentioned the ghost. It simply became a part of the legend of a station that Braide describes as "a great piece of Montreal culture and a legacy of a radio station that meant a lot to a lot of people." When the station relocated down the street to its original location a few years later, the staff held a tongue-in-cheek "Ghostbusters" party to say goodbye to their spectral companion. And that is when the stories of the green-topped ghost seemed to fade, much like the fleeting image of the apparition itself.

However, if you were to go to CHOM-FM's current building and speak with staff from the radio station who had the pleasure of working with Robert "Tootall" Wagenaar over the years, they are likely to tell you that, even though he is now enjoying the disappearing act that comes with retirement, they are very likely to still feel his spirit ever present in that hallowed radio studio.

One Town, Two Poltergeists
Hudson, Quebec

Poltergeists never take credit for their mischief. They work in the quiet, when everyone is out of the room. They move your things around, empty your drawers, break the glass in your picture frames. They are the creak in your floorboards as a chair rocks when nobody is rocking it. They are your bedroom door slamming shut on a windless day. They are here, but you never see them. You see only the mess they leave behind.

In the early 1880s, the town of Hudson, just west of Montreal, was disturbed by two poltergeists, as described by John Robert Colombo in *Ghost Stories of Canada*. The first struck at the Hudson Hotel in October 1880. John Park, the innkeeper, entered a vacant room to find it had been ransacked. All the furniture had been scattered about, including the mattress and the tables and chairs. Weirdly, some pillows had been tied together in such a way that it looked as though a person was sitting there. The windows were all open.

These strange happenings continued for several days. A loaf of bread went missing from the kitchen when the cook left the room briefly. More rooms were left a mess when no one had been there. A fire broke out in the stables. Untouched bottles of booze began to move around in the tavern. The mayhem came to an end rather anticlimactically when a priest performed an exorcism of the building and sprinkled some holy water. There were no further disturbances. All was quiet in the town of Hudson, until it wasn't.

A year later, in May 1881, the Perrault home was rocked with a series of odd disturbances that couldn't be explained by the residents, including Madame Perrault, her five children, her mother, and her grandmother. The disturbances consisted mainly of the quiet shuffling around of objects in the home: a lady's shawl moved, cupboards opened and their contents scattered, furniture toppled. Sometimes it seemed that the poltergeist had a woman's sensibility, because it kept laying things out neatly: a Sunday dress, a roll of lace, winding sheets. Other times there seemed to be some meaning to the disorder, even though that meaning sometimes couldn't be discerned, as when twelve porcelain religious figures were found lying in a circle with their heads all pointed together, as if to make a wheel. Or when two pillows were laid out on a bed and a quilt carefully laid over them, making the pillows look like a covered corpse.

No one ever heard a thing, and they couldn't figure out why any of the events were taking place. Madame Perrault believed that her husband, who was working in Rivière-du-Loup, had passed away and his spirit was haunting them. But her husband was not dead. Then, thirteen-year-old Ernestine, one of Madame Perrault's daughters, began to have convulsions (or "fits") so violent that two grown men could barely hold her down. During one hour-long fit she punched through a pane of glass without cutting her skin. She remembered nothing that had happened during the convulsion once it was over.

A priest was called, and he decided to do a little experiment to see for himself if the stories were true. Herding everyone out of the house, he made sure one room was clean and tidy, then closed the door to be sure no one could get in. A little while later, when he returned to check, the room was a mess.

We can't be sure how things turned out for the Perrault family. No further reports can be found about their home and its poltergeist, though Colombo does put forth one theory that could explain what happened. In the village it was widely known and believed that a curse had been placed on the Perrault family by an old woman. It seemed her husband was owed four dollars for some work he had done for Mr. Perrault, and since he was never paid, the old woman had cursed the house. The villagers seemed unconcerned, asserting that it could have been much worse than furniture being overturned. They believed the old woman could summon Satan.

What happened to the Hudson poltergeist? Were there one or two? Were they banished by the will of the local priest, or did the Perrault family finally pay their debt? We may never know. A poltergeist tells no tales. It simply knocks over your chairs, plays your piano, and locks you out of the house before whisking itself away, leaving you scratching your head, in this case for centuries to come.

The McGill Student Who Killed Houdini
The Princess Theatre, Downtown Montreal

Harry Houdini was born in Budapest on March 24, 1874, and he died in Detroit on October 31, 1926. But the man, whose birth name was Erik Weisz (later Ehrich Weiss, finally adopting his well-known name when he began his career as a professional performer) sealed his fate in Montreal on Friday October 22, 1926, due to a series of sucker-punches he received from a McGill University student by the name of J. Gordon Whitehead.

In a 2004 book titled *The Man Who Killed Houdini*, Don Bell tells the story of that event. He spent almost twenty years speaking to eyewitnesses and gathering the research to tell a very full and thorough tale about the man responsible for the death of someone who was, perhaps, the world's most famous and legendary escape artist, magician, and illusionist.

Bell documents the many different interviews and conversations he had with various people, sharing in detail the conflicting accounts from multiple sources about the specific time, place, and circumstances surrounding the escape artist's infamous demise. Among the tales, Bell stitches together multiple accounts to create a document about Houdini's death, but also the man behind the legend.

According to Bell, Whitehead, along with two colleagues by the names of Samuel "Smiley" Smilovitz and Jacques Prince, entered Houdini's dressing room prior to one of the illusionist's Montreal performances.

There they found the magician reclining on a couch. After some conversation in which Houdini remarked about the abilities of the human body to prepare for intense physical feats, such as being able to withstand a strong blow to the stomach, Whitehead unexpectedly hit Houdini in the stomach, landing at least two, if not as many as four or five, hard punches. Since he was still lying down and not expecting it, Houdini had not been prepared for the series of sucker punches he received.

Almost immediately after the attack, Houdini began to suffer from severe abdominal pain. Nevertheless, as a man who rarely let physical pain or discomfort prevent him from performing (prior to his Montreal stint, he had performed a show in Albany with a broken ankle), he continued on with his scheduled shows at the Princess Theatre that night and the next day.

Montreal's *Daily Star* theatre critic described the performance, which took place in front of an "audience that packed every corner of the edifice." For three hours, they watched with undivided attention "the feats of that master-magician, Houdini, as he gave them a display of legerdemain, illusions, mysteries and the most astonishing of tricks, concluding with an exposé of the fraudulent spiritist mediums who batten upon a gullible public."

This publicity shot shows famed boxer Jack Dempsey pretending to throw a punch at Harry Houdini, who is being held by Benny Leonard.

Following his Saturday performance, Houdini and his entourage boarded a train for Detroit. Despite the terrible agony he continued to experience, he knew there was no time for rest because of the two-week booking at Detroit's Garrick Theater.

Although he collapsed in the wings, overwhelmed by high fever and pain, Houdini continued to perform. Afterward, he was rushed to Grace Hospital in Detroit and diagnosed with acute appendicitis. Two separate operations were performed on him, but the poison from his ailment had already seeped into his blood and he was diagnosed with streptococcus peritonitis. On the afternoon of Halloween in 1926, Houdini whispered to his brother Theo, who had been standing at the man's bedside, "I'm tired of fighting, Dash. I guess this thing is going to get me," and, shortly after, succumbed.

There continued to be debate in the medical community about whether or not the severe blows could have caused the affliction that killed Houdini. But it is entirely possible that the pain from the hard punches he received might have masked the underlying pain from the appendicitis, and, inadvertently, delayed the prognosis. There was also some speculation that the popular showman's ongoing tirade against fraudulent spiritualists might have angered the local medium community enough to make them hire a student like Whitehead to viciously attack the magician.

It was determined that Whitehead was probably nothing more than a hot-tempered young student trying to prove a point … a point that had consequences well beyond that fateful moment. Most historical accounts report that Whitehead simply seemed to drop off the face of the earth, but Bell, in his decades-long research, managed to track down a number of details about the man.

Jack and Frances Rodick, owners of a Montreal bookshop, relayed how one evening in the shop Whitehead had shared with them that the incident was a sad and irresponsible moment that truly haunted him. "When he told us about his involvement in punching Houdini," Frances Rodick said, "I didn't think he intended what happened but he wanted to show Houdini up. Like 'Is that what you think? Then I'll show you!' And of course he did hit him."

"I felt," Jack Rodick said, "that as a student he might have been brash about this sort of escapade, but afterwards he didn't seem at all proud of it."

"Whitehead may have felt like he committed a terrible crime," Frances concluded. "I certainly sensed a deep sadness, and it was probably what made him ill."

Whitehead died sick, troubled, and "thin as a reed," living in a dark apartment surrounded by gigantic piles of magazines and newspapers, which he kept arranging and rearranging in different locations. He was described, by the few people who knew him, as a gentleman and intellectual. He, perhaps, lived the remainder of his life in the shadow of the knowledge that his youthful actions as a McGill student might have resulted in the death of a man whose legacy continues to astonish people from around the world.

The Knotty Poltergeist
The McGill Ghetto, Plateau-Mont-Royal

You may have already smiled at what you think may be a "naughty" typo in the title of this chapter. Or perhaps you enjoyed the cheeky play on words because you are already familiar with the paranormal mystery that has, for almost one hundred years, plagued a home on Prince Arthur Street between Sainte-Famille Street and Parc Avenue.

This particular mystery, believed to be a poltergeist, doesn't involve the usual "noisy spirit" phenomenon — loud noises, knocking over of furniture, or the levitation or throwing of objects by unseen hands. Instead, it involves the appearance of unexplained knots. The phenomenon began in 1929, as outlined in Pat Hancock's 2003 book *Haunted Canada: True Ghost Stories*, with knots that appeared in curtains, towels, sheets, pillowcases, articles of clothing, and various other fabrics throughout the home.

The family was unable to explain the bizarre occurrences, and were soon frustrated with the fact that virtually anything in the home that could be twisted into a knot was tied into ones that were small and tight. Convinced that one of the children was tying the knots, the parents kept a close eye on them. They were, however, unable to find anything amiss in their kids' behaviour. At a loss for a reasonable explanation, they then turned their suspicions upon one another.

But still, no human culprit could be detected.

At their wit's end, they eventually contacted a local journalist as well as a local church, wondering if the home needed to be blessed in order to rid it of the mischievous spirit or spirits at work. Nearby St. Patrick's Church sent two priests to the home. They performed an exorcism ritual in an attempt to dispel the spirit or spirits from the building. But the attempted exorcism of the ghost was fruitless. One of the family members allegedly informed a local journalist that they were told that somebody must have cast a spell on the home.

Finally, not sure what to do next, the family reached out to the local police. When the officers arrived at the family's home, police did a quick search of the house and then interviewed each member of the family individually to determine if anyone had been lying or deceiving the others with a prank. But the interrogations left them baffled and with no clear answers. The police then searched the house again, examining everything thoroughly. They didn't find anything in most of the house, but one of the officers did detect what was described as a foul odour coming from the basement. There was speculation that a body might have been buried there and that that could account for the haunting activity in the home. But after digging up the basement and searching, the police couldn't find any evidence of a skeleton or decomposing body, which might have explained the eerie phenomenon and the odd smell.

Before leaving the home that night, they left a number of handkerchiefs in a room and locked it behind them, sealing the room with police tape to ensure that nobody could enter it. When they returned the next morning, they broke the seal and entered the room, shocked to discover that all of the handkerchiefs had been knotted.

At that point, they again interviewed each of the family members separately, this time providing them with a piece of fabric and asking them to tie a knot in it. They compared each family member's knot with the knots from the sealed room. They determined that the knots created by the family's youngest daughter looked quite similar to the knots from the locked room. They speculated that perhaps this young girl tied them in a "trance-like" state and left that as the final conclusion from their investigation.

Although the chapter in Pat Hancock's book suggests that the knot phenomenon stopped shortly after the family moved out of the home, a

September 2016 article on the Haunted Montreal site explores the phenomenon in a bit more detail and speculates about multiple possibilities for the strange occurrences, including looking at the history of the neighbourhood. Sharing tales of deaths that occurred in the nearby Hôtel-Dieu Hospital and the abandoned original location of the D'Arcy McGee High School — allegedly haunted by McGee himself (assassinated in Ottawa in 1868) — the article speculates that the paranormal activity could be the result of any number of nearby spirits still trapped on this earth. It also goes on to outline that the haunting was first reported in 1929, just around the time the stock market crashed and an unprecedented number of suicides occurred when businessmen and stock brokers suddenly lost everything.

An unidentified elderly man who lived on the street where the knot phenomenon occurred said that people still talk about the mystery to this day. "Because nobody knows the exact address of the poltergeist house, it has always been a bit of a game or a pastime to look for knots in the curtains of the windows of the homes to try and solve the mystery. Long before Pokémon Go started irritating people, we have had to deal with endless Peeping Toms on our street in search of those cursed knots. Many of the residents tired of it and replaced their curtains with blinds and shutters."

It is interesting how something unexplainable and eerie that happened almost ninety years ago has now turned into an activity for curious tourists. Apparently, this poltergeist from 1929 ended up creating a phenomenon that continues to tie people in knots.

Very Little Rest for These Mount Royal Spirits

Mount Royal Cemetery

T he Protestant Mount Royal Cemetery, established in 1852 and situated high on the mountain, is sometimes described as a "city of the dead" overlooking a city of the living. It is also often cited as one of the most haunted locations in Montreal.

Originally intended to serve Montreal's English-speaking community, the cemetery is now the last resting place of more than 160,000 people. But the site's most famous resident is one who is definitely not at rest. Indeed, he has been regularly seen standing watch near the Camillien Houde lookout. The silent figure, often seen standing guard on the edge of the cliffs, is believed to be the spirit of an Algonquin warrior. The man, whose presence very likely precedes the establishment of the cemetery by thousands of years, does nothing mischievous. He merely stands and appears to look over the landscape below. But the mere presence of this silent sentinel is said to have terrorized sightseeing tourists, who have spotted him upon looking up at the cliffs from the aforementioned lookout.

Two different articles on the Haunted Montreal website discuss both the spirit of this mysterious man as well as other eerie spectres and unexplained phenomenon experienced near the cemetery. A July 2016 blog post outlines a number of odd accidental falls from the lookout, as well as a mysterious orb of light.

In 2012, a forty-eight-year-old American tourist fell to his death at approximately 1:00 a.m. His body was discovered at the bottom of a one hundred foot drop after rescuers were called by the man's friends, who reported him missing. The police indicated that no foul play or alcohol seemed to be involved in the incident, and the cause of the man's fall could not be determined.

A few years later a similar thing happened at approximately the same early morning hour. A man, who had been drinking with two friends, fell from the lookout and tumbled down the slope. His two female companions, who tried to help him get back up, ended up also losing their footing and falling down the same slope. All three were injured but survived. They needed to be rescued by a specialized climbing team from the Montreal Fire Department.

Is there a mysterious force lurking in the area from the nearby cemetery, pushing at people with unseen hands?

It seems to be more than a solitary ghost. The same article mentions a man who reported an odd visual phenomenon from near the lookout. Sitting in his car, he was shocked to see a strange orb, ten feet around and alight, floating in the air above his parked vehicle. The ball of light hovered there for several minutes before slowly moving its way east. Uncertain as to whether or not it was a UFO or some sort of spiritual manifestation from the nearby cemetery, the man was confused and frightened by the incident.

A December 2016 blog post on the same site shared tales not only of strange shadowy figures seen lurking in the cemetery after dark, but also fairies and other supernatural entities.

Teams of paranormal investigators, intrigued by the legends of ghostly shadows seen flitting about the graveyard, have descended upon the cemetery over the years. Some of them have reported unexplained ghostly images appearing in the photographs taken during their investigation. These odd images weren't visible to the photographer at the time, but, rather, appeared in the image afterwards. Others shared that they had heard the eerie sound of a little girl giggling and noted that the trees swaying in the wind above their heads sounded uncannily like the sound of a coffin lid opening. Other investigators claimed that they saw fairies dancing about the graves in the cold dark shadows of the night.

In an anonymous letter to Haunted Montreal, a former Westmount High School student wrote that they had experienced something quite disturbing after taking a walk through the cemetery. The student shared that they had returned home after being at the Mount Royal Cemetery and had quickly fallen asleep. A few hours later, they awoke to the eerie sound of a voice repeatedly calling out their name. It appeared to be coming from a male figure who was standing in the dark right there in the person's bedroom. They could apparently make out the shadow of this figure and promptly told it to go away. Terrified and soaked in sweat, the person then describes finding the courage to reach for and turn on the bedside light, only to find there was nobody there. They attributed the experience to perhaps being a spirit who followed them home from the graveyard.

Among the many stories shared about the Protestant Mount Royal Cemetery, one thing seems to be certain: There appears to be little actual rest taking place in this lush, beautifully landscaped 165-acre cemetery.

Locked Up for an Eternity: Haunted Montreal Prisons

Historically, prisons have been places of darkness, filled with the cries of pain from torture, isolation, and near starvation, where atrocities are committed upon the guilty, the insane, and even those wrongly incarcerated. They were places where death from exposure and inhumane forms of torture, not to mention from government-sanctioned executions, regularly occurred. If ever one were to imagine a place that might be rife with lingering and tortured spirits, a prison would surely be at the top of that list.

Below, we include a few Montreal and area prison stories that are sure to unshackle unpleasant thoughts about those prisoners who are locked up for all of eternity.

The Dungeon of Old Montreal Prison

Vauquelin Square (or Place Vauquelin in French), is an urban square located in Old Montreal. It is named in honour of Jean Vauquelin, a naval officer, who was recognized for the bravery he displayed in battle during the Seven Years' War. The square was not always a public space, however — it was the site of the Old Montreal Prison until 1836.

The prison was demolished in 1950 and a courthouse was erected on that spot. Outside the courthouse is the square. Today, tourists flock to the site to check out the beautiful fountain of Neptune, god of the sea (the original name for the square was Neptune Square), and the nearby City Hall. Few among these are aware of the secrets that lay just below the street's surface.

A dungeon and a series of repurposed jail cells still lie underground, rumoured to be haunted by the ghosts of notorious prisoners who were once held in those very cells, some of them awaiting execution.

City workers who access the cells for storage and other purposes have reported feelings of intense claustrophobia, an unexplainable shortness of breath, and overwhelming feelings of dread and fear when moving about the historic corridors. Others report hearing the muffled sound of disembodied voices, the clanking of chains, or a sudden drop in temperature in quickly manifesting cold spots.

Executions in this location began in 1812. The final execution, which occurred in August 1833, was of Adolphus Dewey (written about in detail in the following chapter, "The Last Hanging"). Conditions at the prison were described in the book *History of the Montreal Prison From A.D. 1784 to A.D. 1886* as inhumane, and several of the punishment and torture techniques employed would, by today's standards, be seen as completely barbaric.

A blog post from the Haunted Montreal website speculates that some of the phenomenon experienced in the old underground cells and galleries could be pointing to the ghost of the starving vagrant John Collins, who froze to death in the dungeon in December of 1835. Or perhaps it's the ghost of Adolphus Dewey, who suffered a long and tortuous death, or any other of the executed prisoners, such as the thirteen-year-old B. Clement, hanged for stealing a cow.

When you stand in that square, can you feel the weight of the macabre history of that location, the overwhelming emotion of dread coming upon you, and, perhaps, the faint echoes of the cries of long-ago prisoners?

Pied-du-Courant Prison

Pied-du-Courant Prison is a popular location for visiting ghost hunters and paranormal explorers, and a reminder of one of the more violent chapters in the history of Montreal.

Originally built as a replacement for the Old Montreal Prison, the building operated as a prison from 1836 to 1912. In 1912 the building was acquired by the SAQ (Société des alcools du Québec), the provincially run liquor board. When it closed down, Pied-du-Courant Prison was replaced by the Bordeaux Prison, which is still operational. The largest prison in Quebec, it has a capacity for 1,189 inmates.

Initially created to hold about 276 prisoners, Pied-du-Courant Prison ended up holding more than 1,500 prisoners captured during the 1837–1838 rebellion — hundreds more than even the more modern, larger Bordeaux Prison could handle. The overcrowding and deplorable conditions in the prison must have been unbearable for both the prisoners and those who worked there.

In 2003, a museum called La-Prison-des-Patriotes Exhibition Centre was opened in the basement of the building. It allows visitors to wander some of the subterranean prison cells and learn about the failed rebellion of 1837–1838. It is within this museum and on the grounds outside that apparitions of prisoners and executed men have been reported. Rumours also abound about undocumented prisoners whose bodies were buried in unmarked graves about the prison grounds during the years of overcrowding.

Unexplained mists, mysterious shadowy figures, and the echo of phantom footsteps have been reported by staff and visitors. Visitors have reported feelings of unease, the certainty that they are not alone, and the sudden onslaught of violent thoughts. Objects have disappeared and then reappeared on their own, doors and windows close and open by themselves, and there have been inexplicable electrical disturbances — odd flickering lights and power surges that couldn't be traced to a physical cause.

In June of 2013, Isabelle Verge of the *Journal de Montréal* interviewed a paranormal specialist and author by the name of Christian Paige, who explained to her that the prison, where a dozen patriots were executed, was one of the most haunted sites in Montreal. He suggested that the ghosts of the Patriotes were at "unrest" because they were seeking the justice that escaped them in life. Paige also explained that the location was not only haunted by the ghosts of former prisoners, but also by those of former prison guards.

When a psychic visited the facility, she saw the figure of a ghost, dressed all in blue, running quickly through the prison. "It was a figure which kept running the same line over and over again, always at the same place and in the same direction," she said in a Haunted Montreal blog post from August 2016, "restarting at the same location (similar to a movie just being played on tape)." She couldn't tell if it was a prisoner or a guard, but said she could make out that he was dressed in blue and was running very quickly.

Reading these stories, would you be brave enough to venture underground to explore this haunted historic location? If you do, just ignore that fleeting glimpse of what appears to be the spectre of a prisoner. It's likely just your imagination.

Vieille Prison of Trois-Rivières

Built in 1822, the Vieille Prison of Trois-Rivières, located about one and a half hours from Montreal, was designed to hold about forty prisoners and remained in operation until 1986. Over the years, it was the "home" for some of Quebec's most dangerous criminals.

Once the longest-running detention centre in Canada, the old prison, which has remained almost unchanged since it was created, is a part of Canada's national prison heritage and a major attraction. Visitors can, during a one hour and fifteen minute tour, experience what life was like behind bars in those early days of our country's history. Children twelve and under are not allowed on this harrowing experience. The museum also has a "Sentenced to One Night" program (where no one under the age of fifteen is allowed). Visitors who sign up for this program are greeted by the warden, then they are booked, fingerprinted, photographed, and issued a prisoner's T-shirt. The warden then guides the visitors to the incarceration wing, where a former inmate will recount details of penal life of yesterday and today. Visitors then spend the night with their cellmates under the warden's supervision before waking to clean the wing and eat a meagre breakfast before being given the much-anticipated RELEASED stamp on their hands and set free.

There are those who claim that this prison, like many others, is haunted by former inmates and guards. During the Halloween season of 2017, the museum added special Haunted House tours of the prison, playing up the history of the building with a few additional "just for fun" scares thrown in. We're not sure just how "fun" being in a prison, especially an allegedly haunted prison, might be. But, as the French saying goes: *à chacun son goût* (to each his own taste).

* * *

While modern prisons might be significantly safer and cleaner, and certainly nowhere near as barbaric as some of the overcrowded prisons of the past, prisons are still places of darkness, of reduced freedom; places to be avoided. For those unlucky enough to find themselves in prison, and even more unlucky to die there, freedom may never be possible. As the tales that we have shared make clear, some prisoners have found themselves forever confined to these haunted grounds, with their spirits lingering on for an eternity of torture, fear, pain, and angst.

The Last Hanging:
The Crimes of Adolphus Dewey
Vauquelin Square, Old Montreal

T he last man to be hanged at the prison that once stood on Vauquelin Square in Old Montreal died on August 30, 1833. His name was Adolphus Dewey. Perhaps best known as the man who found God in prison, and whose last words were recorded by evangelist Nancy Towle in a volume titled *Some of the Writings and Last Sentences of Adolphus Dewey*, he was also a jealous man and brutal murderer who would one day haunt the fields where ten thousand spectators came to watch his hanging.

Let us introduce you to Adolphus Dewey. As described on the Old Port ghost walk conducted by Montreal Ghosts, Dewey was a tall and handsome man, brimming with the charm of the Irish. At twenty-three, he was already the owner of a bakery located on Saint-Paul Street in what is now Old Montreal.

It was love at first sight when Dewey met Euphrosine Martineau, a young woman known as the most beautiful girl in the city. Their courtship was brief, with an engagement and marriage quickly following. And there, at the very beginning of their life together, is where their happiness ended. As the owner of a business, Dewey worked six days a week, leaving his wife alone and lonely at home. She was an easy target for those anxious to ruin her marriage. The young French-Canadian men of the area were less than thrilled that an Irishman had claimed the prettiest girl they knew, and when they came to realize he wasn't caring for her as he should, they started a rumour or two about the Dewey marriage. Before long, Martineau was having one affair, then two, then more than two. Though none of these claims were substantiated, when Dewey caught wind of the news, he was furious, and his jealous nature took over. He started beating his wife, and before long Martineau packed her bags and fled back to her father's house.

Dewey regretted his actions after his wife left him, but his jealousy continued to simmer. A week after Martineau's departure, Dewey showed up at the door of his father-in-law's house with his tail between his legs to beg his wife to return to him. Not quite convinced of his contrition, Martineau agreed to attend Mass with Dewey, but stressed that she was agreeing to nothing more. It was a decision that would be her undoing.

After church, Dewey convinced Martineau that he needed to stop by the bakery before taking her home. Once inside the bakery, he locked the door behind him. Martineau, oblivious to the danger she was in, explained to Dewey that she was willing to live with him, but only if they also lived with her father, in case Dewey tried to hit her again. Very calmly, Dewey replied that she needn't worry about their living arrangements, because she was about to die.

Then he grabbed an axe.

The attack was nearly averted when the astonished Martineau threw herself into her husband's arms, an action that resulted in the initial strike missing her entirely. But Dewey would not be thwarted so easily. Reaching into his pocket, he drew out a razor and cut Martineau's throat. Without waiting for her final death throes, he went right out the door, locked it behind him, and jumped in a waiting carriage, which he'd hired to flee the country.

Left bleeding profusely and all alone, Martineau somehow found the strength to crawl to the back door, unbolt it, and drag herself to the shop next door. When the servants opened the door, the sight of the young woman drenched in blood scared them so much they ran. The neighbour, a Mr. Roy, quickly sent for a doctor. After having her wounds stiched closed, Martineau moved to her father's home to recover. Sadly,

The Champ-de-Mars park where Adolphus Dewey's ghost roams. The remains of Montreal's fortifications can be seen here.

strong as she was, Martineau perished ten days later of her wounds, as did the baby growing inside of her. Adolphus Dewey was now being sought for both murder and infanticide.

Dewey was apprehended in Plattsburgh, New York, and sent back to Montreal for trial. His incarceration and trial (which lasted only one day) received international attention and has been called the highest-profile murder trial in nineteenth-century Montreal. The attention the trial received was due mainly to the extreme cruelty and bloodiness of the murder, as well as the young woman's pregnancy.

Dewey spent four months in chains in his cell in a Montreal penitentiary known for its inhumane conditions. It was there that he became suddenly devout, and spent most of his days reading the Bible and praying. One the day of his trial, a huge crowd fought to get into the courtroom to see Dewey, dressed in mourning clothes, with his three lawyers. Though Dewey's legal team tried to convince the jury that he wasn't guilty due to mental derangement, after two dozen witnesses were called against him, it took the jury only fifteen minutes to declare him guilty.

Everyone came to the hanging, which was one of the most popular in Montreal's history. The Champ-de-Mars fields, which currently stretch out behind the Old Montreal Courthouse (now City Hall) and the Palais de Justice de Montréal, were at the time a terrific place to view executions taking place by the walls of the prison. King claims it was known as the best place in the British Empire to see a hanging, and families would often pack a picnic and bring their children to the event.

Dewey wore a black suit for his execution and gave a speech on the scaffold to the enormous crowd. He apologized for his crime, spoke of God, and asked that the crowd pray for him. The hanging itself was gruesome and long, due to the fact that Dewey's neck didn't break when he fell. In a grim parallel to his wife's prolonged death, Dewey twisted on the rope for a good four minutes, frothing at the mouth while ten thousand citizens watched.

Champ-de-Mars is now a picturesque park. Little evidence of the ghastly deaths that once occurred there remain. That is, unless you decide to walk there at night, when you might be approached by the good-natured ghost of Adolphus Dewey, who is known to give much needed advice to those who are down on their luck. One hundred and eighty-five years later, he haunts the grounds where he came to his bitter end, still trying to make up for his terrible crime. Or, perhaps, he is still trying to convince the people of Montreal that he isn't the monster we all know he was.

A Timeline of Tragedies: Historic Violence, Massacres, and Disasters

W hen researching a book like this, there are always those interesting stories that lack the detail or support to warrant a full chapter. We occasionally have to abandon those pieces in favour of longer tales with more details to share. However, sometimes there is a theme that runs through some of these shorter pieces, something that provides the thread to sew them together. Combined with a few of the longer items, these can be made into a cohesive chapter that follows a particular theme.

This chapter is a showcase for some such stories and provides a simple timeline of some of the various historical violent incidents, massacres, and disasters, both natural and man-made, that have occurred in Montreal. They show the breadth of tragedies that have befallen the city over the centuries.

* * *

The history of Montreal goes back a long time, long before the arrival of Europeans in the sixteenth century. The land known today as the City of Montreal was inhabited for two thousand years by Haudenosaunee, Wyandot, and Algonquin. Early Algonquin oral history denotes Montreal as "The First Stopping Place" as part of their journey from the Atlantic coast.

When Jacques Cartier arrived in 1535 he renamed the Hochelaga River the St. Lawrence River in honour of the Roman martyr and saint. He also bestowed a new name on the mountain that lies in the heart of Montreal, calling it "Mont Royal" in honour of King Francis I of France. It is believed that the name of Montreal was derived from that. Cartier's reception by a St. Lawrence Iroquoians nation was a positive one (see "The Missing Village of Hochelaga"). But not all interactions from that point forward were positive. Throughout the city's early history, there were conflicts and massacres.

Almost seventy years later, Samuel de Champlain built a temporary fort and established a fur-trading post. He would have had no way of knowing that the "temporary" structure would eventually host a population of over six hundred colonists as Fort Ville-Marie (built in 1642), and, eventually, the sprawling metropolis of the City of Montreal.

Champlain would also not have foreseen the bloody battles that would take place on the land, nor some of the tragedies that would befall it. Below is a brief timeline of some of those, with a few additional details:

The Flood of 1642

The steel cross on Mount Royal, which continues to be a significant attraction for visitors to the city, was erected in 1924. But the original cross that it replaced was a wooden one, put there on January 6, 1643, by Paul de Chomeday de Maisonneuve in order to thank God for sparing the local population of the village of Montreal, which had been founded in May 1642.

Shortly after the city's founding, an unexpected spring-type thaw in December resulted in massive flooding of the land along the St. Lawrence River. The rising flood waters were a real threat to the people of the village. De Maisonneuve prayed to the Virgin Mary to spare the people of Montreal and promised, if his prayers were answered, to erect a cross on a nearby mountain.

After the flood waters retreated, as if in answer to his prayers, he did as he had promised and erected the wooden cross that was replaced more than two hundred and eighty years later.

Bloody Battles and War with the Haudenosaunee

Prior to the arrival of Europeans and the establishment of the fur trade, war among Indigenous nations had a purpose other than the slaughter of one's enemy. The Haudenosaunee, for example, treated the loss of life and the consolation of a loved one as significant. Due to a belief that the death of a family member had the effect of weakening the spiritual strength of the survivors, it was critical to replace the lost person with a substitute by raiding neighbouring groups in search of captives.

In 1609 Samuel de Champlain recorded that he witnessed a number of battles between the Haudenosaunee and the Algonquin in which very few deaths occurred. This aligned with the understanding that the main purpose of war for the Haudenosaunee was to take prisoners. For the Haudenosaunee, death in battle was avoided at all costs, because of their belief that the souls of those killed in battle were destined to spend the rest of eternity as angry ghosts wandering about in search of vengeance. In fighting against the French, they developed tactics of a quick retreat and setting up stealthy ambush attacks.

During what is known as the Lachine Massacre in 1689, Haudenosaunee warriors launched a surprise attack on the settlement of Lachine, which was located at the lower end of Montreal Island. Here is a description of the attack from the book *Ville-Marie, Or, Sketches of Montreal: Past and Present*:

> During the night of 5th of August 1400 Iroquois traverse the Lake St. Louis, and disembarked silently on the upper part of the island. Before daybreak next morning the invaders had taken their station at Lachine, in platoons around every house within the radius of several leagues. The inmates were buried in sleep — soon to be the dreamless sleep that knows no waking, for many of them. The Iroquois only waited for a signal from their leaders to make the attack. It was given. In a short space the doors and the windows of the dwelling were broken in; the sleepers dragged from their beds; men, women and children, all struggling in the hands of their

butchers. Such houses as the savages cannot force their way into, they fire; and as the flames reach the persons of those within, intolerable pain drives them forth to meet death beyond the threshold, from beings who know no pity. The fiendish murderers forced parents to throw their children into the flames. Two hundred persons were burnt alive; others died after prolonged torture. Many were reserved to perish similarly at a future time. The fair island upon the sun shone brightly erewhile, was lighted up by fires of woe; houses, plantations, and crops were reduced to ashes, while the ground reeked with blood up to a short league from Montreal.

The description above appears quite brutal. But, of course, because most of the penned accounts of the attack were written by surviving French settlers, and there appears to be no written accounts from the Haudenosaunee perspective, one must consider them to be biased.

The Great Earthquakes

At approximately 11:00 a.m. on September 16, 1732, a 5.8 magnitude earthquake destroyed major parts of Montreal. Nearly 190 buildings and 300 homes were damaged in both the initial quake and the fires that followed. According to one report (which can't be confirmed), despite all this destruction only a single person, a young girl, perished.

In an attempt to further investigate this great earthquake, the authors encountered the description of what appears to be a tremendous earthquake that occurred in the same area perhaps fifty years earlier. The following excerpt from Alfred Sandham's 1870 book *Ville-Marie, Or, Sketches of Montreal: Past and Present* describes what appears to be a different earthquake that occurred around the year 1663. The detail is taken from an account by the local Jesuits. We found this particular excerpt to be quite the vivid description, without any concern for over-statement or hyperbole.

About half-past five in the evening of 5th February a great noise was heard throughout all Canada, which terrified the inhabitants so much that they ran out of their houses. The roofs of the buildings were shaken with great violence, and the houses appeared as if falling to the ground. There were to be seen animals flying in every direction; children crying and screaming in the streets; men and women seized with affright, stood horror-struck with the dreadful scene before them, unable to move, and ignorant where to fly for refuge from the danger. Some threw themselves upon their knees on the snow, crossing their breasts, and calling on the saints to deliver them from the dangers by which they were surrounded. Others pass the rest of the dreadful night in prayer; for the earthquake ceased not, but continued at short intervals, with a certain undulating impulse, resembling the waves of the ocean; and the same sensations, or sickness at the stomach, was felt during the shocks, as is experienced in a vessel at sea.

The violence of the earthquake was greatest in the forests, where it appeared as if there was a battle raging between the trees; for not only their branches were destroyed, but even their trunks are said to have been detached from their places, and dashed against each other with great violence and confusion — so much so that the Indians declared that all the trees were drunk. The war also seemed to be carried on between the mountains, some of which were torn from their beds and thrown upon others, leaving immense chasms in the places from whence they had issued, and the very trees with which they were covered sunk down, leaving only their tops above the surface of the earth; others were completely overturned, their branches buried in the ground, and the roots only remaining above ground. During this wreck of nature, the ice, upwards of six feet thick, was rent and thrown up in large pieces, and from the openings, in many parts, there issued thick clouds of smoke, or fountains of dirt and sand, which spouted to a considerable height. The springs were either choked up or impregnated with sulphur; many rivers were totally lost; others were diverted from their course; and their waters entirely corrupted. Some of them became yellow, some red, and the St. Lawrence appeared entirely white, as far down as Tadoussac. This extraordinary phenomenon must astonish those who know the size of the river, and the immense body of water in various parts, which must have required such an abundance of matter to whiten it. They write from Montreal, that during the earthquake, they plainly saw the stakes of the palisades jump up as if they had been dancing; and that of two doors in the same room, one opened and the other shut of their own accord; that the chimneys and tops of the houses bent like branches of trees agitated by the wind; that when they went to walk they felt the earth following them, and rising at every step they took.

From Three Rivers they write, that the first shock was the most violent, and commenced with a noise resembling thunder. The houses were agitated in the same manner as the tops of trees during a tempest, with a noise as if fire was crackling in the garrets. The shock lasted half an hour, or rather better, though its greatest force was properly not more than a quarter of an hour; and we believe there was not a single shock which did not cause the earth to open more or less.

As for the rest, we have remarked, that though the earthquake continued almost without intermission, yet it was not always of an equal violence. Sometimes it was like the pitching of a large vessel which dragged heavily at her anchors; and it was this motion which occasioned many to have a giddiness in their heads. At other times, the motion was hurried and irregular, creating sudden jerks, some of which were exceedingly violent; but the most common was a slight, tremulous motion, which occurred frequently with little noise.

At Tadousac the effect of the earthquake was not less violent than in other places: and such a heavy shower of volcanic ashes fell in that neighbourhood, particularly in the River St. Lawrence, that the waters were as violently agitated as during a tempest. Lower down, towards Point Alouettes, an entire forest of considerable extend, was loosened from the shore, and slid in the St. Lawrence.

There are three circumstances which rendered this earthquake quite remarkable; the first, its duration, it having continued from February to August. It is true the shocks were not always equally violent. The second circumstance relates to the extent of the earthquake. It was universal throughout the whole of New France from Gaspé, at the mouth of the St. Lawrence, to beyond Montreal, also in New England, Acadia, and other places more remote. It must, therefore, have extended more than 600 miles in length, and 800 in breadth. Hence, 180,000 square miles of land were convulsed in the same day, and at the same moment. The third circumstance, which appears the most remarkable of all, regards the extraordinary protection of Divine Providence, which was extended to the inhabitants, for while large chasms were opened in various places, and the whole face of the country was convulsed, yet there was not a single life lost, nor a single person harmed in any way.

We found it interesting that both historic accounts, though they each discuss what appear to be different earth-shattering incidents, include references to significantly far-reaching damage, and yet no (or perhaps only a single) human casualty. Could this seeming miracle have anything to do with the cross erected in 1643?

Cholera and Typhus Epidemics (1832 and 1847)

Most of Lower Canada experienced a large scale Cholera epidemic that began in the summer of 1832 (as also described in the chapter "Cholera Ghosts and Un-Ghosts"). In just a matter of days, the reported death toll was more than two hundred and sixty people, and the final death toll is said to have reached approximately two thousand in Montreal.

But that particular epidemic was perhaps just a warm-up for a disease that struck in the following decade. The typhus epidemic of 1847 was linked with the Great Famine, which was caused by potato blight in Ireland between 1845 and 1849. A large-scale Irish emigration on over-crowded, disease-ridden ships led to the death of more than 20,000 people in Canada, including an estimated 3,500 to 6,000 immigrants, who died of this "ship fever" in Montreal's fever sheds on Windmill Point. (See more about the fever sheds in the chapter "The Heroic Death of John Easton Mills.")

The Great Fire of 1852

No sooner had Montreal recovered from the mass typhus deaths than a fire that originated at Brown's Tavern on St. Lawrence broke out, leaving more than ten thousand people homeless (almost one fifth of the city's population at the time), and destroying half of the city's housing. The spark that lit the fire occurred, unfortunately, when the city's recently constructed water reservoir had been drained and closed for repairs.

The Great Inundation of 1861

The City of Montreal has long been a victim of floods, particularly because of the ice that regularly stops up the St. Lawrence River. But the "Great Inundation of 1861" was a particularly significant one, as can be seen in this excerpt from Alfred Sandham's 1870 book *Ville-Marie, Or, Sketches of Montreal: Past and Present*:

The inhabitants of the lower parts of the city were accustomed to floods, but they were not prepared for such an extensive inundation as that which visited them in the spring of this year. About 7 o'clock on Sunday evening, April 14th, the water rose so rapidly that the inhabitants were unable to remove articles of furniture to a place of safety, and the congregations of St. Stephen's Episcopal Chapel, on Dalhousie-street, and the Ottawa-street Wesleyan Chapel found their places of worship surrounded by four to six feet of water, and no means at hand whereby they might reach their homes. The water rushed so violently down the streets that it was almost impossible to maintain a footing while endeavoring to wade through it. In order to obtain assistance for his congregation, Rev. Mr. Ellegood, of St. Stephen's Church, waded in the dark through about four feet of water until he reached St. Antoine-street. He then procured the assistance of some policemen, and a boat was obtained by which, at about 1 o'clock A.M., the congregation were taken away from the church, with a few exceptions, who stayed all night. The trains from the west and from Lachine were unable to enter the city, and passengers had to find their way to the city by Sherbrooke-street. The principal loss to the inhabitants was in livestock. About 3 o'clock on Monday the pot ash inspection stores took fire from the heating of a quantity of lime. While endeavoring to quench the flames the firemen were standing or wading waist-deep in water. The efforts of the brigade were unavailing, and the building was entirely consumed.

The extend of the inundation may be conceived from the fact that the river rose about twenty-four feet above its average level. The whole of St. Paul-street and up McGill-street to St. Maurice-street, and from thence to the limits of the city, was entirely submerged, and boats ascended McGill-street as far as St. Paul-street. To add to the sufferings of the people the thermometer sank rapidly, and a violent and bitter snow-storm set in on Tuesday, and continued to rage with great fury all night. Owing to the fact that in most cases the fuel was entirely under water much extreme suffering was caused. Considering the rapidity with which the waters rose, it is strange that no more than three lives were lost. These were drowned by the upsetting of a boat, in which they were endeavoring to reach the city. The flood extended over one-fourth part of the city.

Just a few paragraphs later, the text describes the effect of a hurricane that passed over the city in July of that year, creating havoc, tearing down fences and trees, and completely destroying the roofs of the Grand Trunk Railway sheds at Point St. Charles. As with the earthquakes described earlier, all of this seemingly occurred without casualties. In another eerie echo of the earthquakes, July also saw two additional earth-tremor shocks that only lasted a few seconds, but were severe enough to shake buildings and send people rushing out in a panic to the streets.

The "Red Death" Smallpox Epidemic of 1885

In March 1885 a train arrived from Chicago that introduced a plague of smallpox upon Montreal. The disease was transmitted via conductor George Longley, who arrived with an intense fever and a disturbing mass of welts on his face, upper body, and hands.

By the following month, it became evident that smallpox had taken hold of the Montreal General Hospital. A little more than a year later, the disease had infected as many as nine thousand Montrealers, killing more than three thousand and seriously disfiguring countless others.

The real tragedy is that all of this could have been avoided with a simple vaccination, which had been developed in 1796 and was readily available. A good majority of French Canadians, however, were suspicious of the vaccination due to confusing propaganda from the Catholic Church, which included calling those promoting the vaccination "charlatans" and insisting that vaccination was a ploy to poison their children.

The "Saddest Fire" at Laurier Palace

On Sunday January 9, 1927, a horrific and tragic fire broke out in the Laurier Palace Theatre on Saint Catherine Street. The theatre was filled with eight hundred children attending a comedy show. Seventy eight children died in the fire: sixty-four from asphyxiation, twelve who were trampled to death in the ensuing panic, and two from the actual fire itself. It is believed that a hastily discarded cigarette that fell between the theatre's wooden floorboards was the cause of this tragic fire.

Following this tragedy, the public demanded that children be forbidden from attending the cinema, citing the obvious dangers. Judge Louis Boyer recommended that nobody under the age of sixteen should be allowed access to the cinema. That law remained in effect until 1961. In 1967 the cinema law was adapted into a motion picture rating system that divided audiences into age groups — an interesting by-product of that early theatre tragedy.

Trans-Canada Airlines Flight 831

In what was, at the time, the deadliest airline crash in Canadian history (and currently stands as the third-deadliest behind Swissair Flight 111 and Arrow Air Flight 1285), a Douglas DC-8 crashed about four minutes and twenty miles after take-off, near Ste-Thérèse-de-Blainville. The November 29, 1963, flight, which was bound for Toronto from Montreal, crashed, killing all one hundred and eighteen people on board; one hundred and eleven passengers, and seven crew members.

The only somewhat positive aspect of this story is that traffic congestion on Montreal highways that day led to eight additional passengers failing to arrive at the airport in time to catch that flight.

The actual cause of the crash was difficult to determine, since, at that point, Canadian aircraft were not required to carry voice cockpit recorders. Investigation suggested such possibilities as the jet's pitch trim system, icing, and failure of the vertical gyro.

Conclusion
Why Share Macabre Tales?

I am someone who believes in ghosts.

Heck, I not only believe in ghosts, but I'm afraid of the dark. So why would I be interested in writing books that include ghost stories and other ghastly tales? I have thought about it and been regularly asked the question, but I honestly can't tell you. I *can* tell you that I have always been fascinated with eerie things that linger, hidden in the thick darkness of night, with the awe-inducing and overwhelming fear of the unknown.

A common logical next question from people, upon hearing this, is usually: Have you ever seen a ghost yourself?

I truly can't say.

And that is perhaps because that while I believe in ghosts, I haven't decided for myself what I believe they are. Is a ghost the manifestation of a spirit trapped on earth, a lost soul unable to completely shuck off their mortal coil? Or is a ghost more like the remnants of an intense traumatic moment, filled with the most powerful intensity of human emotion; enough intensity to leave a lasting echo in the fabric of space and time, so that what people are seeing when they see a ghost is more like some sort of video loop of that significant event? Or are ghosts things that are created via particular environmental triggers that stimulate particular elements of the electricity or chemistry that make up our brains and our consciousness?

Perhaps. Perhaps ghosts are sometimes one, sometimes another.

Why do some people see or witness paranormal phenomenon while others do not? I believe that, in the same way that some people have particularly refined or heightened senses, perhaps there are those who are more in tune with a type of sense that can detect either an earth-bound spirit or the ripple of energy bound to a "haunted" location. Think about a sommelier — a trained wine professional who can taste a wine and come up with such complex and detailed tasting notes as "cranberry, birch, cloves and just a back-palate hint of rich earthy tones" while others, like me, merely nod and say something like, "that wine is good; a little sweet, a little fruity." Are there folks who, like a sommelier, can see or detect things that the average person isn't able to?

Perhaps.

One of the reasons I believe in ghosts and that there are people who are more likely to experience ghosts is because I, like Hamlet, believe that there are "more things in heaven and earth … than are dreamt of in your philosophy." There are certain math problems whose answers I just can't see. Elements of physics and chemistry fall outside my ability to comprehend. There are a multitude of languages that other humans speak which I fail to grasp; just as there are computer codes and algorithms that I couldn't even begin to build an understanding of. But just because I can't comprehend or explain those things doesn't mean they don't exist, or that others can't understand them. And, while science hasn't yet offered us any proof of the existence of ghosts or what they might be, it might be something that comes, with time.

Another thing I know is that virtually every culture on this planet has some sort of legend, belief, or religion that includes spirits or spirit-like entities, such as animals or objects. So, I remain open-minded.

However, I am also aware that charlatans exist, those who are more interested in tricking others, either for money or attention. And so, when researching ghosts, I approach each subject with an open mind but a skeptic's reservation. I look for logical or mundane explanations for a phenomenon. Where one is found I do try to shine a light upon it. But I also enjoy the speculation that comes with unsolved mysteries, and the "what if?" questions that sometimes arise.

This book doesn't just talk about ghosts, but also the ghastly events that are often found inside a rich and intriguing ghost story. Think about the beheading and dismemberment of poor Mary Gallagher, whose ghost and legend lingers in Griffintown. Sometimes these ghastly events have no accompanying ghost stories. These tales shock, stun, and disturb us. But, like ghost stories, we are drawn to these dark and nasty tales. Does that make us evil or disturbed? Or is it merely an element of human nature to seek them out? Some might argue that what draws us to pay attention to these types of stories stems from an element of human survival — instinctive behaviour that we have little control over. Truly bad or negative experiences help teach us what's not good for us.

Historically, people do respond in a deeper way to tragedy or darkness. The emotions and memories associated with a dark event seem to imprint themselves in a more intense way than even positive emotions such as joy. For example, let me ask you something that might be meaningful if you are of a certain age. Perhaps part of the Baby Boomer generation.

Where were you when JFK was killed?

If you ask someone who was alive then, they are likely to tell you, in intense detail, where they were, who they were with, how they found out about it. Perhaps if you're closer to my age (I'm in my midforties as I write this) you have a similar experience when reading one of the following questions:

Where were you when U.S. president Ronald Reagan was shot?

What do you remember about the Space Shuttle Challenger explosion?

Or maybe, if you are a bit younger than me, the following questions dredge up rich personal stories or details:

Where were you during 9/11?

Where were you when you learned about the Sandy Hook Elementary School shooting?

Tragedy, disaster, and macabre events stick out in our minds; they plant intense memories that can truly disturb us. But they can also have an effect of bringing people together. When people share personal details about a historic event, they share with one another and feel closer to the people they are with. Traumatic events can also bring out the best in humanity. During 9/11, for example, strangers welcomed displaced travelers into their homes. They can also remind us of the limitless compassion that people can have for one another. And, ultimately, despite the tragic and terrible things that can happen, there can be love and hope, and we can learn from, and hopefully seek to prevent, such tragedies from occurring again.

Shayna and I hope that, in reading this book, we helped you to explore some of the fun and eerie tales that Montreal has to share. We hope that you have gained a new appreciation for a truly world-class Canadian city. Perhaps we have shared a few tales in this book that made you think. Perhaps some of the stories inspired you to keep an extra light on, or had you quivering a little beneath the sheets at some odd and unexplained sound that woke you in the middle of the night. And perhaps after reading something within the pages of this book, we helped you to learn something fascinating about Montreal and its dark, ghastly, and sometimes macabre history, that you came away with a nugget of a story to share at a dinner party or a social event.

I know that, after the intense and fascinating research that we engaged in while collecting these stories, both Shayna and I have a whole new understanding of the richness, the complexity, and the history of the people and places that make Montreal so wonderfully unique.

Mark Leslie

Appendix
More Than Just a Little Fresh Air and an Eerie Perspective:
Haunted Montreal Walking Tours

One of the things that makes the process of putting a book like this together both easier and more pleasurable is being able to share stories with groups that specialize in local hauntings. Walking tour groups allow for an immersive experience, where history and ghostly lore come together through both eyes and ears.

During the research phase for this book, Shayna had the pleasure of going on several of the Haunted Montreal ghost walks in order to get into the proper mood, and for inspiration. As we continued our research, both of us found ourselves returning to the website and blog Haunted Montreal, which were created to share research into ghost sightings, paranormal activities, historic hauntings, and unexplained and strange local legends.

Donovan King, the owner of this company, was not only kind enough to write the foreword to this book, but he also shared with us some of the inspiration and motivation behind wanting to establish such a company in Montreal.

A native of the city, King credits an inspirational high school drama teacher with lighting a fire under him. Then, in 1994, King was unexpectedly bitten by the haunted acting bug when an Oscar award–winning special effects specialist named Robert (Bob) Short was in Montreal to set up a haunted house called Chateau Greystoke.

Donovan King, owner of Haunted Montreal, in character and sharing one of the city's eerie tales.

Appendix

Enjoying this role, King realized that this type of haunted acting was a lot of fun. He described it as having more flexibility, improvisation, and interaction than a standard piece of traditional theatre, and the clients experienced much stronger emotions, usually fear. "It opened my eyes," he says, "to a whole new way of doing theatre!"

In 1995, King moved to London, England, and landed a job at the famous London Dungeon. King worked there for two years, sharpening his skills in the haunted acting genre.

King eventually returned to Canada, spending a few years doing a master's degree in theatre studies in Calgary. When he arrived back in Montreal, he did some smaller haunted projects, including one called Scare Stories. In 2006, not long after King returned to Montreal, he began working for Fantômes Montréal Ghosts, a company that offers Old Montreal ghost walks led by professional actors. This group, formed in 1999, was the first business to develop the concept of evening street performance theatre, with actors performing as ghosts of the past to convey historic knowledge for the audience. (You can learn more at fantommontreal.com.)

King began roaming the mountain and discovered many more ghost stories, soon realizing that there were enough stories to create a ghost tour of the area. He began researching and constructing a script, with the initial idea of conducting it just once for that year's Halloween season. Haunted Montreal began unofficially in 2011 with one ghost tour on Mount Royal in English, which was simply called "Haunted Mountain." When 180 guests showed up, King realized that there was a lot of potential to expand upon.

In 2015, King started the Haunted Montreal blog to begin educating people about Montreal's vast haunted heritage.

Throughout this growth, King has continued to work with Montreal Ghosts, where he gets to share tales in Old Montreal, as well.

"I am very proud to be able to create quality employment while simultaneously sharing a fascinating part of Montreal's history with our residents and visitors. I am also happy to be regarded as one of Canada's leading experts in haunted acting and Montreal ghost stories."

During the editing of this book, the website Haunted Montreal suspended operation for a short period of time. The authors hope this was merely a temporary setback, as the group offers a special richness.

What is certain is that wherever you are, be it in Montreal or another city with a rich and colourful history, you can experience a little bit of creepy, fun, and historic stories with tours offered by groups like Haunted Montreal, Fantômes Montréal Ghosts, and Secret Montreal. You'll get some fresh air and perhaps a fresh and eerie new perspective on the city.

Acknowledgements

Shayna

To begin with I have to thank Mark for being all-in when I casually suggested that we write a book about Montreal ghost stories. Your confidence in my writing and your support mean so much to me, and I'm so glad we were able to do this project together.

Thank you so much to all the folks at Dundurn who made this book come together. As a novice to the process of getting a book published in print, I feel so lucky to have the opportunity to work with such engaged and delightful people, who want this book to succeed as much as I do.

Thanks to my buddy Terri, who happily took on a Montreal ghost walk in my stead and told me all about the creepy tales she heard. More than one chapter in this book would never have come to be without your help.

To Eyal, you are my husband, my partner in crime, my best friend. Thank you for listening to my every worry as I worked through this first non-fiction book, first co-write, first book to come out IN PRINT. You never let me forget what a big deal this is, even if I did, and you took care of our little guy while I struggled to meet my deadlines. You make me feel all the schmees.

To anyone who picks up this book and enjoys our collection of spooky tales, just know how much it means to me that you're spending your hard-earned dollars on our work. A ghost story only exists if it is told, and the telling means nothing without a listener. So, thanks for listening.

Mark

I have had the distinct pleasure of working with Shayna at my day job from 2011 until 2017. Apart from talking about work things, Shayna and I often bonded over our passion for writing and elements of our ongoing dances with the muse. But when she first suggested the idea of a collaboration on a book of ghost stories about Montreal, I was intrigued. Oh, who am I kidding, she had me at the first word in her pitch.

Little did I know that this writing collaboration would allow me to continue to have the pleasure of working with Shayna well after I moved on to pursue different writing and publishing pursuits. I'm thankful for the continued teamwork and collaboration we got to experience together, in particular those much needed "kick-in-the-pants" texts from Shayna whenever I was required to pick up the pace on my half of the book. In all seriousness, Shayna made this project fun, intriguing, and another pleasurable way to explore and get to love a city that I thought I knew.

The folks behind the scenes at Dundurn deserve a huge nod of thanks for all that they do to support and care for their authors, mostly out of sight of the public eye. Thank you, Dominic, for your guidance and patience during the editing process, for helping tweak my words and thoughts to make them shine, and especially for your patience with my "but" and "let me explain my perspective on this" ramblings through the editing process. Thanks also to Jenny McWha for continued polishing and tweaks and edits to help improve my words. Thanks to Kathryn Lane and Rachel Spence, and the creative team for the work and support with such a beautiful cover and great-looking book. Thank you to Michelle Melski and Heather McLeod for the promotional support. And thank you (and happy retirement) to Sheila Douglas for being on top of keeping us authors feeling listened to and cared for throughout the entire process.

And, of course, there are also those folks whose work on my previous books, even while this one was in process, is still appreciated. Though they are now on new journeys, I bid thanks to Jaclyn Hodson and Margaret Bryant for their support on my previous titles. And I would like to wish a very happy and enjoyable retirement to Beth Bruder, whose stray comment in an industry meeting led to the genesis of my first Dundurn title, *Haunted Hamilton*, all those years ago.

Thank you to Liz, my beautiful partner, for patiently listening to me going on about the historical and eerie research that I was conducting. Thank you, also for joining (and protecting) this big chicken when the chilling tales left me jumping at my own shadow.

And last, thanks to the readers, especially those who take the time to reach out, wanting to share their own eerie stories and tales, for posting reviews, for the comments and support. Your response and enthusiasm related to a book like this help fuel that passion to keep writing and to keep sharing macabre and eerie tales with those who, like me, revel in the dark and spooky.

Sources

Books

Abbot, David Phelps. *Behind the Scenes with the Mediums*. Chicago: Open Court, 1912.

Bell, Don. *The Man Who Killed Houdini*. Montreal: Vehicule Press, 2004.

Chambers Dictionary of the Unexplained. Edinburgh: Chambers Harrap, 2007.

Colombo, John Robert. *Ghost Stories of Canada*. Toronto: Dundurn Press, 2002.

———. *More True Canadian Ghost Stories*. Toronto: Prospero Books, 2005.

Hancock, Pat. *Haunted Canada: True Ghost Stories*. Toronto: Scholastic, 2003.

LeMaster, J.R., and James D. Wilson. *Routledge Encyclopedia of Mark Twain*. New York: Routledge, 2013.

Leslie, Mark. *Tomes of Terror: Haunted Bookstores and Libraries*. Toronto: Dundurn, 2014.

Leslie, Mark, and Rhonda Parrish. *Haunted Hospitals: Eerie Tales About Hospitals, Sanatoriums, and Other Institutions*. Toronto: Dundurn, 2017.

Marlowe, John. *Canadian Mysteries of the Unexplained: Investigations into the Fantastic, the Bizarre and the Disturbing*. London: Acturus, 2011.

Neville, Terry. *The Royal Vic: The Story of Montreal's Royal Victoria Hospital, 1894–1994*. Montreal: McGill-Queen's University Press, 1994.

Norman, Michael, and Beth Scott. *Haunted America*. New York: Tom Doherty, 1994.

Poplak, Lorna. *Drop Dead: A Horrible History of Hanging in Canada*. Toronto: Dundurn, 2017.

Sandham, Alfred. *Ville-Marie, Or, Sketches of Montreal: Past and Present*. Montreal: G. Bishop, 1870.

Schechter, Harold. *The Serial Killer Files: The Who, What, Where, How, and Why of the World's Most Terrifying Murderers*. Toronto: Random House, 2003.

Sneath, Allen Winn. *Brewed in Canada: The Untold Story of Canada's 350-Year-Old Brewing Industry*. Toronto: Dundurn, 2001.

Taft, Charles Sabin. *Abraham Lincoln's Last Hours*. Chicago: Blackcat Press, 1934.

Volo, James M., and Dorothy Deneen Volo. *Family Life in Native America*. Westport: Greenwood Press, 2007.

Articles

"5 High-Profile Montreal Mob Murders." *Maclean's*, August 16, 2012. macleans.ca/society/life/5-high-profile-montreal-mob-murders/.

"10 of the Most Notorious Mobsters in the History of Montreal." MTL Blog, 2016. mtlblog.com/lifestyle/10-of-the-most-notorious-mobsters-in-the-history-of-montreal.

Abley, Mark. "Montreal Is a City of Ghosts." *Montreal Gazette*, October 17, 2014. montrealgazette.com/news/local-news/montreal-is-a-city-of-ghosts.

Bain, Christopher. "Many Close Encounters Predicted for Montreal." *Montreal Gazette*, February 1, 1978.

Baron-Goodman, Sara. "Grey Nun Ghosts and a Murderer's Grave." *Concordian*, October 28, 2014. theconcordian.com/2014/10/grey-nun-ghosts-and-a-murderers-grave/.

Brownstein, Bill. "CHOM's Tootall on Retirement: '40 Years Is a Nice Thing to Shoot For.'" *Montreal Gazette*, September 8, 2017. montrealgazette.com/opinion/columnists/choms-tootall-on-retirement-40-years-is-a-nice-thing-to-shoot-for.

Bruemmer, Rene. "Rousing Ghost of Mount Royal." Global News, October 29, 2010. globalnews.ca/news/100640/rousing-ghost-of-mount-royal/.

Burke, Jim. "Royal Vic and Its Ghosts Come to Life One Last Time in Hospital Farce *Progress!*" *Montreal Gazette*, October 21, 2015.

Cameron, D. Ewan, J.G. Lohrenz, and K.A. Handcock. "The Depatterning Treatment of Schizophrenia." *Comprehensive Psychiatry: Official Journal of the American Psychopathological Association* 3, no. 2 (April 1962).

Carpenter, Phil. "Finding of Willow Inn Ghost Hunt Revealed." Global News, August 13, 2017. globalnews.ca/news/3667043/findings-of-willow-inn-ghost-hunt-revealed/.

"Courdu Coroner — Ada Maria Mills Redpath." Archives Nationales du Quebec — Centre d'archives de Montréal, Ed McMahon. June 14, 1901.

D'Alimonte, Michael. "10 of the Most Horrific Disasters in the History of Montreal." MTL Blog. mtlblog.com/lifestyle/10-of-the-most-horrific-disasters-in-the-history-of-montreal.

Davis, Bruce. "Opinion: Montreal Mayor John Easton Mills Helped the Desperate Migrants of His Time." *Montreal Gazette*, November 11, 2015. montrealgazette.com/news/local-news/opinion-montreal-mayor-john-easton-mills-helped-the-desperate-migrants-of-his-time.

Farber, Michael. "UFO Clerk Blasé About Sightings." *Montreal Gazette*, April 17, 1985.

Farnsworth, Clyde H. "Canada will pay 50's Test Victims." *New York Times*, November 19, 1992.

"How the Hells Angels Slaughtered Five of Its Own in Quebec 30 Years Ago Only to Become More Powerful." *National Post*, March 24, 2015. nationalpost.com/news/canada/how-the-hells-angels-slaughtered-five-of-its-own-in-quebec-30-years-ago-only-to-become-more-powerful.

Kalbfleisch, John. "Cholera Brought Tragedy, and Some Comedy, to Montreal." *Montreal Gazette*, May 26, 2012. montrealgazette.com/sponsored/mtl-375th/from-the-archives-cholera-brought-tragedy-and-some-comedy-to-montreal.

Kelly, Jeanette. "Infinitheatre's Play *Progress!* Celebrates the Royal Vic." CBC, October 18, 2018.

King, Donovan. "The Haunted Trafalgar Tower Site — Part II." *Montreal Times*, January 20, 2016. mtltimes.ca/Montreal/montreal/the-haunted-trafalgar-tower-site-part-ii/.

Lejtenyi, Patrick. "How a Dismembered Montreal Sex Worker Became a Sensation, Then a Ghost, and Now a Fading Legend." VICE, March 1, 2017. vice.com/en_ca/article/8qb9z4/how-a-dismembered-montreal-sex-worker-became-a-sensation-then-a-ghost-and-now-a-fading-legend.

Mariani, Mike. "Nativism, Violence, and the Origins of the Paranoid Style." Slate, March 22, 2017. slate.com/articles/news_and_politics/history/2017/03/the_awful_disclosures_of_maria_monk_and_the_origins_of_the_paranoid_style.html.

"MK-ULTRA Violence; Or, How McGill Pioneered Psychological Torture." *McGill Daily*, September 6, 2012. mcgilldaily.com/2012/09/mk-ultraviolence/.

Morin, Yves, and Philippe Daniel. "Quebec Beer-Drinkers' Cardiomyopathy: Etiological Considerations." *Canadian Medical Association Journal*, vol. 97 (October 7, 1967).

Mota, Chris. "Grey Nuns Leave Motherhouse for Concordia University Takeover." CBC, April 6, 2013.

"Mother and Son Dead." *Globe*, June 14, 1901.

"Mother and Son Shot." *Halifax Morning Herald*, June 14, 1901.

"Murdered with an Axe." *Montreal Weekly Witness*, July 2, 1879.

"Mysterious Shooting." *Calgary Herald*, June 14, 1901.

"Mysterious Tragedy." *Ottawa Morning Citizen*, June 14, 1901.

Novakovich, Jeannette. "Murder at the Redpath Mansion." Montrealités, December 6, 2012. montrealites.ca/crime/2012/12/murder-at-the-redpath-mansion.html.

Principe, Miguel, and Janine Xu. "Murders of Montreal: Stories that Still

Haunt the City." *McGill Tribune,* October 31, 2017. mcgilltribune. com/student-living/ murders-of-montreal-stories-that-still-haunt-the-city-103117/.

"Redpath Tragedy In Montreal." *Quebec Daily Mercury*, June 14, 1901.

Riga, Andy. "A Montreal Mystery: Hunt for Lost Village of Hochelaga Starts on St-Viateur Ave." *Montreal Gazette*, July 6, 2017. montreal gazette.com/news/local-news/a-montreal-mystery-hunt-for-lost-village-of-hochelaga-starts-on-st-viateur-ave.

Sabourin, Diane. "Montreal Planetarium." *Canadian Encyclopedia*, February 2, 2014. thecanadianencyclopedia.ca/en/article/ montreal-planetarium/.

"Sad Occurrence." *Montreal Daily Star*, June 14, 1901.

Schwartz, Susan. "Ottawa Spending $851,000 to Conserve Grey Nuns' Mother House." *Montreal Gazette*, October 12, 2017. montreal gazette.com/news/local-news/ottawa-spending-851000-to-conserve-grey-nuns-mother-house.

———. "Portraits of Montreal's Now-Empty Royal Victoria Hospital." *Montreal Gazette*, November 23, 2017. montrealgazette.com/news/ local-news/portraits-of-montreals-now-empty-royal-victoria-hospital.

Scott, Marian. "Montreal, Refugees and the Irish Famine of 1847." *Montreal Gazette*, August 12, 2017. montrealgazette.com/feature/ montreal-refugees-and-the-irish-famine-of-1847.

———. "Mystery of the Missing Village of Hochelaga Persists." *Montreal Gazette*, February 17, 2015. montrealgazette.com/news/local-news/ mystery-of-the-missing-village-of-hochelaga-persists.

Shabsove, Mia. "This Abandoned Prison Near Montreal Is Transforming into a Terrifying Haunted House for Halloween." MTL Blog, October 2017. mtlblog.com/whats-happening/this-abandoned-prison-near-montreal-is-transforming-into-a-terrifying-haunted-house-for-halloween.

Shivji, Salimah. "Royal Vic in Demand as Movie Set as MUHC Awaits Sale of 19th-Century Hospital." CBC News, May 24, 2016. cbc.ca/ news/canada/montreal/muhc-legacy-sites-royal-victoria-chest-1.3586378.

"Strange Double Life of Mr. Ellis, Hangman." *San Antonio Light*, September 18, 1938.

"Tragedy In Montreal." *New York Times*, June 14, 1901.

Twain, Mark. "Mental Telepathy Again." *Harper's Magazine*, September 1895.

Vanderperre, Julie. "Declassified: Mind Control at McGill." *The McGill Tribune*. mcgilltribune.com/mind-control-mcgill-mk-ultra/.

Websites

"Chasse-galerie." Wikipedia. wikipedia.org/wiki/Chasse-galerie.

"Château Ramezay." *Canadian Encyclopedia*, October 8, 2012. thecanadianencyclopedia.ca/en/article/le-chateau-ramezay/.

"The Château Ramezay." Paranormal Studies & Inquiry Canada. psican. org/index.php/ghosts-a-hauntings/quebec/718-the-chateau-ramezay.

"A Concise History of Montreal." Montreal for 91 Days. http://montreal. for91days.com/a-concise-history-of-montreal/.

"The Curse of the Dow Brewery." Urbex Playground. urbexplayground. com/urbex/curse-dow-brewery.

Dittman, Geoff, and Chris Rutkowski. "UFOs Over Canada: 25 Years of UFO Reports." canadianuforeport.com/survey/UFOsOverCanada.pdf.

"The Dow Brewery in Downtown Montreal, Canada." Montreal Paranormal. http://www.montrealparanormal.com/ps-canada-old-dow-brewery.php.

"Dubois Brothers." Wikipedia. wikipedia.org/wiki/Dubois_Brothers.

Gagné, Michel. "Hochelaga." *Canadian Encylopedia*, February 20, 2013. thecanadianencyclopedia.ca/en/article/hochelaga/.

Gillman, Gary. "Dow Ale — A Great Beer Name with a Sad Ending." Beer et seq, February 1, 2016. beeretseq.com/dow-ale-a-great-beer-name-with-a-sad-ending/.

"Harry Davis (gangster)." Wikipedia. wikipedia.org/wiki/Harry_Davis_(gangster).

Haunted Montreal Blog. Haunted Montreal. hauntedmontrealblog. blogspot.com/2015/06/.

"The History of Judicial Hangings in Britain 1735–1964," Capital Punishment U.K. capitalpunishmentuk.org/hanging1.html.

"Honoré Beaugrand." Wikipedia. wikipedia.org/wiki/Honor%C3%A9_Beaugrand.

"Laurier Palace Theatre." Wikipedia. en.wikipedia.org/wiki/Laurier_Palace_Theatre_fire

"The Mafia of Montreal: A Short History." Gangsters Inc, 2005. gangstersinc.ning.com/profiles/blogs/the-mafia-of-montreal-a-short.

"Maria Monk." *World Heritage Encyclopedia*. Project Gutenberg. gutenberg.us/articles/eng/Maria_Monk.

"Marie-Joseph Angelique." Canadian Encyclopedia, February 18, 2014. thecanadianencyclopedia.ca/en/article/marie-joseph-angelique/.

"Marie-Joseph Angelique: Remembering the Arsonist Slave of Montreal." Activehistory, September 25, 2012. activehistory. ca/2012/09/marie-joseph-angelique-remembering-the-arsonist-slave-of-montreal/#comments.

Marsh, James H. "Plague: The 'Red Death' Strikes Montreal." *Canadian Encyclopedia*, May 2, 2013. thecanadianencyclopedia.ca/en/article/plague-the-red-death-strikes-montreal-feature/.

"Meetup." The Montreal Ghost Tracking Meetup Group Message Board, 2008. meetup.com/ghosts-656/boards/thread/4344631/0/.

"Montreal's Top 10 Gangland Murders: #10 Harry Davis." Coolopolis, October 8, 2011. coolopolis.blogspot.ca/2011/10/montreals-top-10-gangland-murders-10.html.

"The Nastiest Crime Ever to Hit Brossard." Coolopolis, November 22, 2012. coolopolis.blogspot.ca/2012/11/the-nastiest-crime-ever-to-hit-brossard.html.

"Ramezay Castle." Haunted Places. hauntedplaces.org/item/ramezay-castle/.

The Redpath Mansion Mystery. Great Unsolved Mysteries in Canadian History, 2008. canadianmysteries.ca/sites/redpath/home/indexen.html.

"Rizzutos vs. Violis: Mafia War in Montreal." Coolopolis, November 14, 2010. coolopolis.blogspot.ca/2010/11/rizzutos-violis-and-story-of-current.html.

Torture and Truth: Angelique and the Burning of Montreal. Great Un-
    solved Mysteries in Canadian History, 2006. canadianmysteries.ca/
    sites/angelique/accueil/indexen.html.

"Trans-Canada Air Lines Flight 831." Wikipedia. wikipedia.org/wiki/
    Trans-Canada_Air_Lines_Flight_831.

"Wayne Boden." Wikipedia. wikipedia.org/wiki/Wayne_Boden

"Wayne Boden — The Vampire Rapist." Serial Killer Central, July 17,
    2010. serialkillercentral.blogspot.com/2010/07/wayne-boden-
    vampire-rapist.html.

"Wayne Clifford BODEN." Murderpedia. murderpedia.org/male.B/b/
    boden-wayne.htm.

"What is Epilepsy?" Epilepsy.com. epilepsy.com/learn/about-epilepsy-
    basics/what-epilepsy.

"The Willow Inn's Ghost." Hudson Historical Society: Musée
    Hudson Museum. Facebook, June 11, 2015. facebook.com/
    HudsonHistoricalSocietyandMuseum/posts/ 1007153209297305.

Ghost Walks, Videos, and Podcasts

"1990: UFO Phenomenon over Montreal," Newswatch. CBC, November
    7, 1994.

"Beer Deaths in Quebec." This Hour Has Seven Days. CBC, April 3,
    1966. cbc.ca/archives/entry/beer-deaths-in-quebec.

Bloustein Marshall, Jessica. "The Tobogganing Ghost of Montreal."
    WAMC Podcasts, 2017. wamcpodcasts.org/podcast/the-
    tobogganing-ghost-of-montreal/.

Gifford, Larry. "Episode 150." October 27, 2017, in Radio Stuff Podcast.
    soundcloud.com/radio-stuff-podcast/episode-150-ghostly-
    radio-tales.

"Ghost Walk and Dark Encounters." Montreal Ghosts. Talk, October 29,
    2017.

"Haunted Downtown Ghost Walk." Haunted Montreal. Talk, October
    30, 2017.

"Haunted Griffintown Ghost Walk." Haunted Montreal. Talk, October 20, 2017.

"Haunted Griffintown Tour & McLennan Library Ghost." Haunted Montreal. Talk, October 13, 2015.

"Haunted Mountain Ghost Walk." Haunted Montreal. Talk, November 3, 2017.

"MK Ultra." *The Fifth Estate*. CBC, March 11, 1980.

"MK-ULTRA Survivor Speaks." YouTube, November 30, 2011. youtube.com/watch?v=zJ6Jg1ztKZg.

Image Credits

Book Credits
Developmental Editor: Dominic Farrell
Editor: Jenny McWha
Proofreader: Jennifer Dinsmore

Cover and Interior Designer: Laura Boyle

Publicist: Elham Ali

Dundurn
Publisher: J. Kirk Howard
Vice-President: Carl A. Brand
Editorial Director: Kathryn Lane
Artistic Director: Laura Boyle
Director of Sales and Marketing: Synora Van Drine
Publicity Manager: Michelle Melski

Editorial: Allison Hirst, Dominic Farrell, Jenny McWha, Rachel Spence, Elena Radic
Marketing and Publicity: Kendra Martin, Kathryn Bassett, Elham Ali

dundurn.com   dundurnpress
@dundurnpress   dundurnpress
dundurnpress   info@dundurn.com

FIND US ON NETGALLEY & GOODREADS TOO!

DUNDURN